PHILADELPHIA QUAKERS

1681-1981

Philadelphia Yearly Meeting, which embraces 113 Monthly Meetings in parts of
Pennsylvania, New Jersey, Delaware and Maryland, gathers annually in the
double meeting house at Fourth and Arch Streets, Philadelphia. This is the home
also of the Monthly Meeting of Friends of Philadelphia. It was built in 1804.

PHILADELPHIA QUAKERS
1681-1981

ROBERT H. WILSON

DESIGN BY RAYMOND A. BALLINGER

A Tercentenary Family Album

PHILADELPHIA YEARLY MEETING

of the

Religious Society of Friends

Committee for Publication

ELEANOR STABLER CLARKE   BARBARA L. CURTIS
H. MATHER LIPPINCOTT, JR.   DANIEL D. TEST, JR.
FRANCIS G. BROWN

Sources of many illustrations are indicated.
Special photography by Theodore B. Hetzel, Thomas J. Laverty,
Otto V. Maya and the late Charles P. Mills, Jr.
Photographs of Twelfth Street/George School Meeting House
from Hayes & Hough, architects.

Printing by Smith-Edwards-Dunlap Company

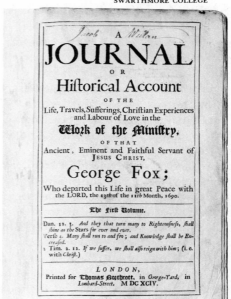

First edition of George Fox's journal

QUAKERS

Members of the Religious Society of Friends have been called Quakers since 1650. George Fox, the founder tells the origin of the name in his journal, first published in 1694.

Fox had been sentenced to six months in jail for "the avowed uttering and broaching of divers blasphemous opinions contrary to a late Act of Parliament." The prison keeper was "plagued" with regret, Fox relates, and went to tell the justices who had pronounced sentence . . .

> *"And one of the Justices replied (as he reported to me) that the plagues were on them too, for keeping me. This was Justice Bennett, of Darby, who was the first that called us Quakers because I bid them 'Tremble at the Word of the Lord'. And this was in the Year 1650."*

THE FIRST QUAKERS IN AMERICA

English Quakers began coming to America 25 years before William Penn's "Holy Experiment" began in Pennsylvania in 1681.

The first to cross the ocean were not settlers with families seeking homes in the new world. They were individual Quaker preachers, traveling ministers fired with zeal to spread "Truth." And those who arrived first were women.

Elizabeth Harris visited Maryland in 1656, traveling from place to place holding meetings for Quaker worship wherever she could find hearers. In that same year, two other Quaker women, Ann Austin and Mary Fisher, reached the port of Boston intent upon the spread of Quaker teaching in Massachusetts Bay Colony, but Puritan clergymen had been forewarned about "the cursed set of heretics called Quakers" and would not let the women speak. They were arrested and held in jail until they could be shipped back on the same vessel which brought them. Their Quaker books and pamphlets were burned by the public hangman.

Other Quaker missionaries arrived with such frequency that authorities began inflicting more and more severe penalties, particularly in Massachusetts. A law in Maryland decreed arrest and whipping for "vagabonds and idle persons known by the name of Quakers." In Boston some Quakers had ears cut off, and four were hanged—Mary Dyer, William Robinson, Marmaduke Stephenson and William Leddra. Their crime was not so much their personal religious beliefs as their fierce persistence in returning time after time to preach in places from which they had been banished under pain of death.

In a few early settlements Quakers escaped harassment and, particularly in Rhode Island, were welcomed in the name of religious freedom. Quaker settlements developed in such places, and meetings for worship went uninterrupted. The first Yearly Meeting of Friends in America was organized in Newport in 1671. Half-yearly "general" meetings were held on the shores of the Chesapeake in 1672, eventually developing into Baltimore Yearly Meeting, the second in the colonies.

Quaker settlements flourished in the 1670s on Long Island and in the northern portion of New Jersey (then called East Jersey). But at that time, the future home of Philadelphia Yearly Meeting was still largely an unsettled wilderness.

A statue of Mary Dyer, one of four Quakers hanged in Boston, sits quietly on a bench as if in Meeting for Worship. Near the entrance to Philadelphia's Friends Center, it is the work of the late Quaker sculptress Sylvia Shaw Judson.

GEORGE FOX IN DELAWARE VALLEY

George Fox himself made a religious visit to the American colonies in 1672-73. Arriving first in Maryland, he held meetings there with Friends, with other English settlers and with Indian chiefs. He reported many convinced by the precepts of Quakerism, including community leaders whom he identified loosely as "magistrates" or "governors." His journal tells of attending a five-day meeting in Maryland at a place on the Tred Avon River called Betty's Cove.

> *"There were so many, besides Friends, that it is thought there were sometimes a thousand people at one of these meetings. Although they had not long before enlarged their meeting place and made it as large again as it was before, it would not contain the people.*
>
> *"I went by boat every day four or five miles to it, and there were so many boats at that time passing upon the river that it was almost like the Thames."*

After months in the southern colony, Fox traveled north to spend other busy months in East Jersey, New York, Connecticut and Rhode Island. He attended the Yearly Meeting in Newport. He spent days at a time in the homes of prominent Friends and spoke day after day at meetings for worship. When his mission there was ended, he undertook the long, difficult trek south again on horseback. His Journal describes in vivid detail the wild country he found in the Delaware Valley.

First, headed north, he made his way to "the Dutch town of Newcastle," then crossed to the Jersey side of the Delaware River:

> *"Then we had that wilderness country to pass through since called West Jersey. We travelled a whole day together without seeing man or woman, house or dwelling place. Sometimes we lay in the woods by a fire, and sometimes in Indian wigwams or houses."*

Later, traveling south, Fox reached the Delaware at about the present site of Burlington, New Jersey, and decided "to pass through the woods on the other side."

> *"We swam our horses over a river about a mile wide, at twice, first to an island called Upper Didinock, and then to the mainland; having hired Indians to help us over in their canoes.*
>
> *"This day we could reach but about thirty miles and came at night to a Swede's house, where we got a little straw and lay there that night. Next day, having hired another guide, we travelled about forty miles through the woods, and made us a fire at night by which we lay and dried ourselves; for we were often wet in our travels."*

Months later, when Fox arrived back in England, one of the first to meet with him was 29-year-old William Penn, already a leader among English Quakers. Fox visited in Penn's home. No doubt the minds of both men were influenced by thoughts of the vast unsettled territory along both sides of the Delaware River in contrast to the steady development of Quaker settlements north and south.

QUAKER SETTLEMENT IN "WEST JERSEY"

The southern portion of New Jersey became a Quaker colony before Pennsylvania was created. William Penn had much to do with it.

"The Jerseys" had been the property of John Lord Berkeley and Sir George Carteret, but in 1674 Berkeley put his holdings up for sale, providing an opportunity for Quakers encouraging emigration to America. Apparently for the benefit of the Society as a whole, Berkeley's land was purchased in the names of two Friends, Edward Billinge, a London merchant, and John Fenwick, a retired career soldier.

Differences arose between these two inexperienced proprietors, and William Penn was asked to serve as arbitrator rather than have the matter litigated in court. In the settlement, Billinge became owner of nine-tenths of "West Jersey" and Fenwick of one-tenth. "East Jersey" to the north remained in possession of Carteret.

Fenwick immediately began efforts to sell sections of his land to Quaker settlers, but Billinge ran into financial difficulties. William Penn was again called upon to straighten out matters as one of the trustees for the creditors. Half a dozen years before he applied to the King for a province of his own, Penn was supervising the sale of land for Quaker settlement in Jersey.

He and the other trustees published literature describing opportunities for emigration and promising special treatment for members of the Society of Friends:

> *"The disposal of so great a part of this country being in our hands, we did in real tenderness and regard to Friends, and especially the poor and necessitous, make Friends the first offer— that if any of them, though particularly those that being low in the world and under trials about a comfortable livelihood for themselves and families, should be desirous of dealing for any part or parcel thereof, that they might have the refusal."*

MARY W. SMITH

The great oak tree under which Fenwick and his settlers gathered in 1675.

SALEM—THE COLONY OF FENWICK

John Fenwick was quite a different man from William Penn, an aggressive professional soldier who had become a Friend in middle age. He was a contentious character who quarreled with nearly all his associates. He called his one-tenth of the West Jersey land "The Province of Fenwick" and asked settlers to pledge allegiance to him as the head of government.

Along with some fifty purchasers of his land, Fenwick embarked from London in 1675 aboard the ship *Griffin*. They sailed up the Delaware River to the mouth of a large creek with the Indian name Asamhockin. There they began the town which Fenwick called Salem "because of the delightsomeness of the land."

As was to be the case in Pennsylvania a little later, the Quakers of West Jersey met few of the difficulties experienced by pioneer colonists earlier in Virginia or Massachusetts. The land was fertile, the Indians friendly, the climate good. Salem thrived from the very beginning, although Fenwick himself lived only until 1683.

Friends met for worship outdoors or in tents until the first houses were built. Afterwards they met in the log house built by Samuel and Ann Nicholson close by a large white oak tree which is still standing today. Salem Friends Meeting was organized there in 1676, and a few years later the Nicholsons deeded to the Meeting not only the log house but sixteen surrounding acres for a burying ground which still occupies the same spot beneath the spreading branches of the great Salem Oak.

BURLINGTON

When Penn and his fellow trustees assembled 250 Quaker colonists and their families to sail for Jersey in 1677, King Charles went down the Thames on the royal yacht to observe the departure and to wish the voyagers well. These were purchasers of Billinge's land. They sailed in the ship *Kent* and disembarked at nearly the same place on the shore of the Delaware where George Fox had crossed the river five years before.

Many of the Friends in this group came from Bridlington, in Yorkshire, and they chose that name for their new community. But before many years passed, Bridlington became Burlington. Streets were laid out, lots chosen, and houses started. In 1678 Burlington Monthly Meeting of Friends was established.

Plans for a meeting house at Burlington were first made in 1682 and Francis Collins, an experienced builder from England, engaged to build it—a hexagonal structure of brick which was not finished for several years since Collins was busy at the same time erecting the county courthouse.

Burlington's six-sided meeting house, 1686.

ACROSS THE DELAWARE

Not all those who came originally to Salem or Burlington in the 1670s remained on the Jersey side of the Delaware. Some from Salem ventured across the river to live at Chester (then called Upland). Some from Burlington crossed over to establish homes and new Friends meetings at Shackamaxon and "The Falls" (Falsington). Until Pennsylvania came into existence, these first Quaker arrivals, along with the few Swedes and Dutch already on the land, came under the authority of Edmund Andros, Britain's royal Governor of New York.

When William Penn first came to take possession of his province in 1682, he found comfort and hospitality in the large homes of Robert Wade at Chester and Thomas Fairman at Shackamaxon.

ON TRED AVON RIVER

While settlement in West Jersey was beginning, Friends in Maryland were spreading out along the eastern shore of Chesapeake Bay. George Fox in 1672 had attended crowded meetings at Betty's Cove on Tred Avon River.

By 1676, a second Friends meeting had been established on the river. This Tred Avon Meeting constructed a frame meeting house in 1682-84, a small building facing the water and conveniently reached only by boat. At one time the Meeting owned a ferry to make family traveling easier.

Eventually the city of Easton, grew up around the site and separated meeting house from river.

Tred Avon Meeting and its 1682 meeting house have been in continuous existence for three centuries. As generations have passed, the name has gradually evolved from Tred Avon to Tread Haven to Third Haven. But the original meeting house has changed but little, one of the oldest houses of worship in continuous use in the United States.

Since 1790, Third Haven Monthly Meeting has been part of Philadelphia Yearly Meeting.

Third Haven Meeting.

ELEANOR STABLER CLARKE

8

Old photograph taken soon after Third Haven Meeting added a brick meeting house beside the original in 1884. The frame building is still used except in coldest weather.

THE

"HOLY EXPERIMENT"

IN

PENNSYLVANIA

His experience with Quaker settlements in West Jersey encouraged William Penn to petition King Charles II in 1680 to establish a Friends colony on the other side of the Delaware River. The young man had inherited considerable influence at the British court from his late father, Sir Admiral Penn. Moreover, the crown was still indebted to the father's estate for war service against the Dutch. After a year's negotiation, the King on March 4, 1681 signed a royal charter making Penn Proprietor of a huge new province still largely unsettled and lying between older colonies to the north and south.

Thus began the unprecedented Quaker venture for which Penn coined the phrase "Holy Experiment."

> "For my country, I eyed the Lord in the obtaining of it, and more was I drawn inward to look to Him and to owe it to His hand and power, than in any other way.
> "I have so obtained it, and desire that I may not be unworthy of His love, but do that which may answer His kind Providence, and serve His Truth and people; that an example may be set up to the nations; there may be room there, though not here, for such an holy experiment."

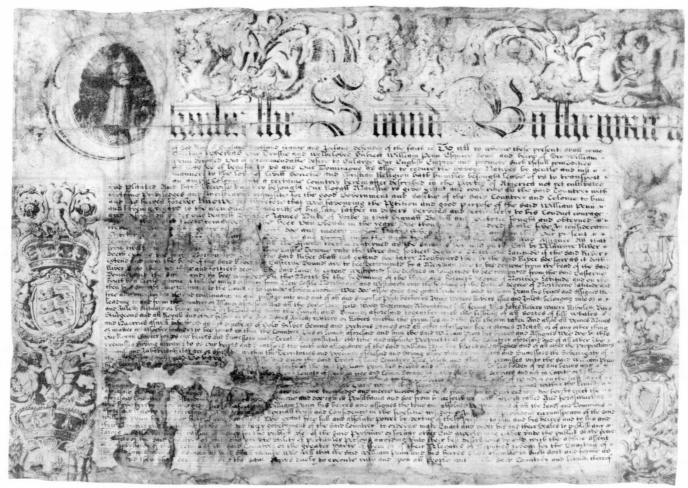

The royal charter granting William Penn his province.

PROPRIETOR AND GOVERNOR

Promptly following the grant of his charter, Penn sent his cousin, William Markham to Pennsylvania as deputy governor to take possession and deliver a letter to the scattered English, Dutch and Swedish families already settled there:

> "My Friends: I wish you all happiness here and hereafter. I have to let you know that it hath pleased God in His Providence to cast you within my lot and care . . . You are now fixt at the mercy of no Governor that comes to make his fortune great; you shall be governed by laws of your own making, and live a free, and, if you will, a sober and industrious people. I shall not usurp the right of any, or oppress his person; God has furnished me with a better resolution . . ."

The Proprietor also sent a letter addressed to "the King or Kings of the Indians in Pennsylvania:"

> "My Friends: There is one Great God and Power that hath made the world and all things therein, to whom you and I and all people owe their being and well-being . . . This Great God hath written His law into our hearts by which we are taught and commanded to love and help and do good to one another and not to do harm and mischief one unto another . . . I shall shortly come to you myself at which time we may more freely and largely confer and discourse of these matters."

To "put power in the people," William Penn drafted a First Frame of Government which he and his first purchasers formally adopted in London before some of them set out for Pennsylvania during 1681. Some others crossed the ocean in early 1682, but Penn himself was unable to sail until he could dispose of a mass of preliminary business. One important matter was to insure Pennsylvania access to the sea. This was accomplished when the King's brother, the Duke of York, deeded to Penn as an addition to Pennsylvania the three "Lower Counties" which now comprise the state of Delaware.

Finally, in early September, 1682, Penn embarked for his province with about 100 Friends, men, women and children, in the ship *Welcome*.

WILLIAM PENN

It is ironic that the best authenticated portrait of the Quaker leader William Penn is one showing him in a suit of armor.

Penn was 22 years old when it was made. He had completed his education and traveled on the continent as befitted a young gentleman of a wealthy and well-connected family. He went to Ireland in 1666 to administer the rich family estates and while there served in the militia, helping to subdue a local insurrection. He was offered command of a company and when he posed in armor for this portrait he may well have been contemplating a military career similar to his father's.

By the next year, however, he had abandoned a promising future at court, had joined the Society of Friends and been jailed for publishing his religious views. While in the Tower of London at age 24 he wrote his best-known book, *No Cross, No Crown*. Despite his youth he became one of the principal leaders of Quakerism, well prepared by his intelligence, his education and his background to help in the settlement of West Jersey and to undertake his "Holy Experiment" in Pennsylvania.

The original of the portrait reproduced here was presented to the Historical Society of Pennsylvania in 1833 by Granville Penn, a grandson. It was one of several copies owned by the Penn family.

HISTORICAL SOCIETY OF PENNSYLVANIA

THE NAME "PENNSYLVANIA"

Neighboring American colonies were already named New York and New Jersey. Penn suggested his province be named New Wales.

> "I chose New Wales being, as this, a pretty hilly country. When the Secretary—a Welshman—refused to have it called New Wales, I proposed Sylvania, and they added Penn to it; and though I much opposed it, and went to the King to have it struck out and altered, he said 'twas past and would take it (responsibility) upon him; nor could twenty guineas move the undersecretaries to vary the name, for I feared lest it should be look't on as a vanity in me, and not as a respect in the King, as it truly was, to my father whom he often mentions with praise."

This world-famous painting does not represent any one historical event, but portrays the spirit in which Quaker William Penn dealt with the American Indians.

Penn negotiated many treaties with the Indians. He met with them frequently during his first visit to Pennsylvania in 1682-84 when he lived at Shackamaxon near the great elm tree which stood on the river bank until 1810. In this painting, Penn appears considerably older than he was at the time represented, and some of the costumes are out of date. But the message of the painting is accurate and authentic.

Benjamin West, the painter, was a birthright Quaker born in a house which is now a faculty residence on the campus of Swarthmore College. He possessed such natural talent that the Friends Meeting laid aside its tenet in opposition to artistic endeavor and joined in helping to further his education. West went abroad to study at age 22 and never returned to America. He became historical painter to the British King.

This painting was completed in London nearly a century after Penn's visits to Pennsylvania. It was executed for the Penn family, and remained in their possession until 1851 when it was purchased and brought to Philadelphia. Since 1878 it has been one of the treasures of the Pennsylvania Academy of the Fine Arts.

PENN AND HIS PROVINCE

Although he lived 37 years after obtaining his province, Penn was unable to spend more than four of them in Pennsylvania. He made two visits, each lasting about two years.

He first sailed up the Delaware in the *Welcome* to land on October 27, 1682 at Newcastle where he established his jurisdiction over the Lower Counties before moving upriver to Chester. When he reached the site selected for his capital city of Philadelphia, streets and lots had already been laid out by his surveyor and a few houses constructed.

Penn lived during that visit at Shackamaxon. Gulielma Penn and their three young children remained at home, expecting to join the Proprietor in Pennsylvania when the affairs of the province permitted. Instead, Penn had to return to London in August, 1684, to defend his interests at court in connection with the Pennsylvania-Maryland boundary line. There was an overlap in the royal grants of Pennsylvania to Penn and of Maryland to Lord Baltimore. Penn had to deal with the problem all the rest of his life.

In London in 1684, the boundary matter was temporarily disposed of, but other difficulties and complications prevented Penn's returning to Pennsylvania for fifteen years. Five months after he reached England, his patron, King Charles II, died to be succeeded by James II. Penn was a close friend and adviser of the new king, with whom he had gone to school. Penn found himself drawn into the crosscurrents of English politics, and when James was driven from the throne in 1688 in favor of William and Mary, Penn for a time faced accusations of treason. He was cleared and lived in semi-retirement writing religious works and making

Quaker missionary journeys through England and on the continent.

Gulielma Penn died in 1694. Two years later Penn married Hannah Callowhill. At last, accompanied by her and his grown daughter, Letitia, Penn was able to sail for Philadelphia in September, 1699. With him at that time also came 25-year-old James Logan, newly hired to be secretary to the Governor.

During this second visit, the Penns lived much of the time at the country estate, Pennsbury, which the Proprietor had planned in 1682-4. Penn had brief opportunity to enjoy the life of a rural squire to which he had so long looked forward. He entertained many visitors there including Indians with whom he completed a number of additional friendly agreements and treaties. When in Philadelphia, Penn lived at the Slate Roof House which his wealthy friend Samuel Carpenter had just completed on Second Street between Chestnut and Walnut. A son, John, was born there in February, 1700.

Slate Roof House.

The major event of this period was the drafting and adoption of the Charter of Liberties and Privileges of 1701. The original Frame of Government for Pennsylvania had been revised several times since 1681, and further changes were needed. Months were spent in discussion with the Assembly and the Executive Council before the new Charter was adopted on October 28. It provided self government and religious freedom to the people of the province, extinguishing virtually all of Penn's powers of government.

Penn was obliged to return to London where Parliament in the face of threatened war was again considering suspending the powers of proprietary governors. He waited only until the new Charter was adopted before embarking with his family for

England. Although he had promised himself a life in "the quietness of a wilderness," he never again saw Pennsylvania.

Penn's last years were burdened by sickness, financial problems, frustration and disappointment because of political squabbles in his province. Trickery by a dishonest steward resulted in his spending nine months in debtors prison rather than pay claims that were fraudulent.

When his health was failing in 1712, Penn negotiated for the sale of his proprietorship to the Queen with a stipulation that she take Quakers under her special care. The terms were agreed upon, but Penn suffered a major stroke before the papers could be completed. He was totally incapacitated, and until his death in 1718, Hannah Callowhill Penn was in fact the Governor of Pennsylvania.

The Pennsylvania proprietorship descended to three Penn sons, John, Thomas and Richard, and continued until the last proprietary Governor, grandson John Penn, was turned out of office in 1776.

Penn's spacious country estate on the Delaware has been most attractively recreated by the State of Pennsylvania from the Founder's own plans and instructions in his correspondence. It is open to the public.

The parchment original of Penn's 1701 Charter of Liberties and Privileges is preserved at the headquarters of the American Philosophical Society in Independence Square. Penn's provisions began: "FIRST: Because no people can be truly happy tho' under the greatest enjoyment of civil liberties, if abridged of the freedom of their consciences as to their religious profession and worship . . . I do hereby grant and declare that no persons inhabiting in this province or territories who shall confess and acknowledge one Almighty God, the Creator, Upholder and Ruler of the world . . . shall be in any case molested or prejudiced in his or their person or estate, because of his or their conscientious persuasion or practice . . ."

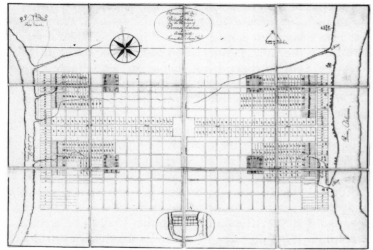

"A Greene Country Towne"

Penn urged that houses in Philadelphia be placed "in the middle of each lot so that there may be ground on each side for gardens or orchards or fields, that it may be a greene Country Towne which will never be burnt, and always be wholesome." This "Portraiture" of the city made in 1683 shows the straight streets and open public squares still in existence in downtown Philadelphia.

15

CALEB PUSEY'S PLANTATION—1683

Long before leaving London, William Penn and his colleagues planned the erection of a mill they knew would be greatly needed in the new province "for the grinding of grain and sawing of boards." Penn and nine other Friends formed a partnership to build and operate it. They chose Caleb Pusey, one of the partners, to be the manager.

When the *Welcome* sailed for Pennsylvania, Pusey was on board with Penn. So was Richard Townsend, builder of the mill. Grindstones, precut timbers and "gears, utensils and implements" were all included in the ship's cargo to facilitate construction.

A woodcut of Caleb Pusey's home.

Richard Townsend's second mill in Germantown was built the year after he put up the Pusey Mill which must have looked much the same.

Caleb Pusey purchased land near Chester on both sides of Chester Creek at the head of tidewater, about two miles upstream from the Delaware River. There his stone house was built in 1683. When it was time to begin building the mill, Penn visited the house, stood in the doorway with Pusey and Townsend and chose its site "forty rods above, in the woods." Townsend lost no time getting it ready for operation. Then he moved northward to build another mill for himself in Germantown in 1684.

Pusey called his place "Landingford Plantation." Travelers journeying north and south crossed Chester Creek only a short distance upstream. Pusey's became a popular stop, especially for Friends making religious visits. Chester Friends Meeting sometimes met in his home.

The Pusey Mill was twice swept away by floods. Reconstruction was so expensive that all the partners dropped out except Penn and Pusey. Their shares were sold at Sheriff auction to Samuel Carpenter, Penn's friend in Philadelphia. When Penn returned to Pennsylvania in 1699,

Built in 1683, this stone cottage has been carefully restored and furnished to appear as it did when William Penn visited and Chester Monthly Meeting gathered before 1700. It stands less than a mile from an interchange of Interstate Highway 95.

the partnership had been reduced to three. A new weathervane with the date and the initials of the trio of owners had been erected on the roof of the mill.

In their later years, Caleb and Ann Pusey retired to London Grove. Landingford Plantation passed through a long succession of owners until acquired by John Price Crozer, who recognized its historical importance. The old mill was destroyed by fire in 1858, but the house remained and Crozer placed its ownership in a trust for the future.

Known locally as "Billy Penn's House," the old stone dwelling became badly neglected. It was in danger of collapse when two historically-minded Quaker women formed The Friends of Caleb Pusey House, Incorporated, in 1960 and began efforts to save it. They obtained wide support and completed both archeological and architectural studies of the structure. Today the dwelling is completely restored, suitably furnished and attractively maintained in a park setting with a museum open to the public.

All that remains of Caleb Pusey's mill is this 1699 weathervane preserved among Penn memorabilia at the Historical Society of Pennsylvania.

GEORGE FOX'S GIFT TO PHILADELPHIA

Perhaps not many modern Philadelphians notice the 16 acres of quiet, undisturbed greenery lying along lower Germantown Avenue surrounded by an impoverished and run-down north city neighborhood. It is the old Fairhill Friends Burying Ground. The land was a 1691 gift of George Fox to the Quakers of Philadelphia.

Although Fox never saw Philadelphia, he had received from William Penn a gift of more than a thousand acres of land. When he died in 1691 he left sixteen acres to the Friends in Philadelphia:

"Ten of it for a close to put Friends horses in when they come afar to the meeting, that they may not be lost in the woods; and the other six for a meeting house, a school house and a burying place, and for a playground for the children of the town to play on . . ."

By the time Fox's estate was settled, Friends had established Fairhill Meeting on the Germantown road, about half way between Philadelphia and Germantown. The land of George Fox became the burying ground.

THE YEARLY MEETING IS ORGANIZED—1681

In the same year William Penn received the King's charter for Pennsylvania, Quakers already settled along the Delaware held the first session of what is now Philadelphia Yearly Meeting.

Burlington began it. Friends at the monthly meeting in the house of John Wolston in May, 1681, recommended that a General or Yearly Meeting be held in Burlington three months later. This was in accordance with the plan George Fox had drawn up for the organization of the Society. Yearly Meetings then, as now, included silent religious worship but were held primarily to attend to the business affairs of the Society and the discipline of its membership.

One of the minutes adopted at the initial Yearly Meeting on August 28, 1681 was to discourage lawsuits between members:

> *"It is agreed if any difference do arise between any professing the Truth that they do not go to law with one another before endeavor has been made and used for the ending thereof by the particular Monthly Meetings they belong to."*

A second Yearly Meeting came together in Burlington in 1682 by which time some of Philadelphia's first Quaker settlers were already arriving. It was reported that William Penn would soon be coming to establish Pennsylvania, but there was not yet a Monthly Meeting in Philadelphia, and the city did not participate in the Yearly Meeting.

This letter of caution was sent to the four Monthly Meetings represented:

> *"Friends: This is writ for Truth's sake by way of advice from the General Meeting that male and female both young and old . . . may all take heed that they be not found in wearing superfluity of apparel nor immoderate nor unseemly taking tobacco, also selling of needless things whereby any may take occasion of offense justly, but that we all may be found to be kept within the bounds of moderation and within the limits of the spirit of Truth and may be known to be governed by the Truth in all concerns."*

By the time of the third Yearly Meeting in 1683, Philadelphia Monthly Meeting had been organized and its representatives were present at Burlington along with Governor Penn himself. Penn and five others were delegated "to write to the Yearly Meeting of Friends in England in order to give an account of the affairs of Truth here . . ."

Friends in Philadelphia soon outnumbered those of the meetings in West Jersey. A second Yearly Meeting for Pennsylvania was considered, but it was decided instead "that there be but one Yearly Meeting in the Province of West Jersey one year at Burlington and another at Philadelphia." For the next 65 years, Yearly Meeting alternated from one side of the river to the other. Its name became The Yearly Meeting of Friends in Pennsylvania, West Jersey and adjoining Provinces. Finally, in 1760, the Yearly Meeting was permanently located in Philadelphia.

THE BANK MEETING HOUSE

QUAKER COLLECTION, HAVERFORD COLLEGE LIBRARY

Friends had two meeting houses under construction in Philadelphia in 1685. One was a frame building on North Front Street above Arch, the other a brick meeting house in Center Square about where City Hall now stands.

The original intention was that the one in Center Square would be the principal place of worship, with the other serving primarily for afternoon meetings. But the city did not develop westward as rapidly as expected. Center Square proved inconvenient, and after a few years the meeting house there was torn down. The property was sold back to William Penn. He, in turn, gave the bricks and other building material to the Philadelphia Meeting to be used to rebuild the frame structure on Front Street.

Located on a slight hill above the Delaware, this early meeting house was referred to as being "on the front of Delaware" or "on Delaware side" and eventually became known simply as "The Bank Meeting House."

After 1685, Yearly Meetings alternated between the six-sided meeting house at Burlington and the Bank Meeting House in Philadelphia.

WILLIAM PENN WAS HERE

The first meeting houses built in the city of Philadelphia were torn down and replaced long ago, but several in the surrounding countryside are still in use after nearly three centuries. Old Haverford Meeting House was begun in 1693, with additions in 1700 and 1800. The original section remains. Merion Meeting built a log house in 1683 and replaced it in 1695 with the stone meeting house which is used today. William Penn attended meetings for worship in both.

Old Haverford Meeting House.

Merion Meeting House—1695.

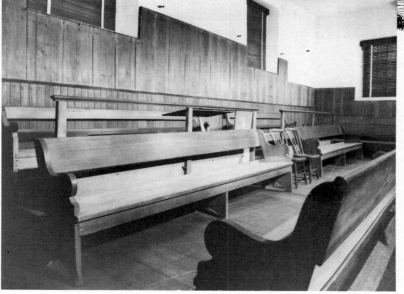

After hearing William Penn tell of his first visit to Pennsylvania, Elizabeth Simms, a Quaker servant in his household, decided she herself would like to live in the new province. Thanks to her, Philadelphia Monthly Meeting now has available to it a million-dollar trust fund for the aid of "Friends in necessitous circumstances."

Elizabeth Simms had been with the Penns for nine years. They encouraged her to emigrate to Pennsylvania, gave her introductions to prominent Friends in Philadelphia and made it possible for her to become owner of a town lot on Walnut Street near Third as well as considerable acreage in the countryside. She came to Philadelphia in 1685 and within a year was married under the care of Monthly Meeting to John Martin, a tailor.

The couple built a tiny house on the rear of the Walnut Street lot. It faced the passageway which is now called Willings Alley. When Elizabeth died in 1699, John Martin became owner, living there alone until his death in 1702. During his final years he was cared for by fellow members of the Meeting.

• • •

In appreciation for the assistance he had received, John Martin gave his property in trust to three members of Philadelphia Monthly Meeting to be used "for poor members of the Society of Friends." The Meeting permitted needy families to live there rent free, and in 1713 built half a dozen similar cottages on the property for the same purpose. Each family lived separately in its own quarters, those who were able taking day-time jobs to help with expenses.

About 1728, the Meeting built the Friends Almshouse along the Walnut Street frontage of the Simms-Martin lot, a large structure providing individual rooms for women Friends in need. The Almshouse concept was so unusual for its time that distinguished visitors to the city were regularly taken to see it. Later, largely at the insistence of Friends in the municipal government, the city built the first public almshouse.

The cottages in the courtyard behind the Almshouse remained in use. A passageway called "Walnut Place" ran directly through the Almshouse to enable residents to reach them.

• • •

In the course of time, newer facilities for the care of needy Friends were developed. The Almshouse and the cottages behind it disappeared and the Meeting put up a 19th Century office building, using the revenue from it to help provide other accommodations for dependent members. Finally, in 1924,

The cottage at the rear of Elizabeth Simm's lot near 3d and Walnut Streets, Philadelphia—1695.

Friends Almshouse—1728
When Saint Joseph Chapel, the first place of Catholic worship in Philadelphia, was built next door to the Almshouse, this home for impoverished women became known as "The Quaker Nunnery."

Friends sold the entire Simms-Martin property and the new owners put up the present building.

If you study the structure at 320 Walnut Street today you will notice it has a hooded doorway quite different from the entrances to most office buildings. Inside, a wide corridor runs all the way through the first floor to an open courtyard on Willings Alley at the rear. The words "Walnut Place" appear on the front of the building over the doorway. A thoughtful architect has left these reminders of the property's historic past.

• • •

A committee of seven members of Philadelphia Monthly Meeting holds the proceeds of the sale of the real estate and other assets of John Martin in trust for the benefit of "necessitous cases" referred by monthly meetings in the Philadelphia area. The committee makes distributions through monthly meetings rather than directly to individual members. Although three centuries ago helping needy Friends meant primarily providing residential shelter and food, today the John Martin trust helps in many other ways to meet more complex problems of twentieth-century living.

An office building today still carries reminders of a Quaker heritage going back to 1685.

Hoping to strengthen his proprietorship claim in the boundary dispute with Lord Baltimore, William Penn encouraged Quaker settlement to the south and sold about 18,000 acres lying along the old Indian trail from Chester to the Susquehanna River. These were known as the Nottingham lots. A Quaker community grew up, and several Friends Meetings were established. When the border was finally established at the line drawn by English surveyors Charles Mason and Jeremiah Dixon in 1767, however, most of the Nottingham lots proved to be in Maryland, as we are reminded by this Maryland highway marker.

East Nottingham and West Nottingham Friends Meetings became part of Baltimore Yearly Meeting. Colora Monthly Meeting, established much later near Calvert, Maryland, however, is attached to the Western Quarter of Philadelphia Yearly Meeting.

Colora Meeting House.

GREENWICH IN FENWICK COLONY

John Fenwick's plans for his colony included in addition to Salem a second town located near the mouth of Cohansey River and named Greenwich. (Today it is still called Green-wich). Before it was fairly started, John Fenwick died and Greenwich remained a quiet, pleasant little settlement which seems today quite far removed from the twentieth century.

The main thoroughfare leading to Greenwich is still designated Ye Greate Street. The first meeting house of logs was built there in 1687. A 1779 brick meeting house near the water's edge is not now actively used, Friends worshipping today in a smaller one at "Head of Greenwich" at the other end of Ye Greate Street.

LOWER ALLOWAY'S CREEK MEETING

Some of Fenwick's early Quaker settlers established homes along Alloway's Creek in the fertile flat country below Salem. Meetings for worship were held in Friends homes as early as 1678 and a meeting house was built in 1684 on the north side of the creek. This proved inconvenient for a majority of the members living on the other side and a second meeting house was built on the south bank in 1710. In turn, it was replaced in 1753 by the brick meeting house still standing. This has undergone fewer changes perhaps than any of those remaining from colonial days.

The bricks of Alloway's Creek meeting house are made of native clay held by mortar fashioned with oyster shells from nearby Delaware River. The interior woodwork is original; the pegged benches are made of yellow pine which disappeared long ago from South Jersey. Bench cushions are homespun linen, some filled with wool, some with corn husks. The shutters which divide the building in two are swung by ropes from the ceiling. The stoves are made of New Jersey bog iron which never rusts.

MARY W. SMITH

22

The original Haddon Field, built 1713, destroyed by fire 1842.

ELIZABETH HADDON OF HADDONFIELD

After John Haddon, a wealthy London Quaker, bought numerous tracts of West Jersey land for investment purposes, he decided not to come to America and permitted his 20-year-old daughter to come as his agent.

After workmen were sent ahead to build a home, the youthful Elizabeth Haddon arrived in 1701 equipped with a power of attorney empowering her to negotiate sale or lease of any of her father's property. She brought with her a widow friend of the family as companion and two men servants. She lived first at Newton and belonged to Newton Friends Meeting organized in 1682.

John Estaugh, a traveling Friends minister from England, arrived in Jersey about the same time as Elizabeth. They were married about a year later under the care of Newton Meeting. In 1713 they built a substantial home on the Cooper River and called it Haddon Field, a name which subsequently spread to Haddon Township and to the modern Borough of Haddonfield.

Elizabeth Haddon Estaugh was clerk of Women's Monthly Meeting for more than fifty years. She and her husband traveled widely in the Quaker ministry until his death on a religious visitation to Tortola in the West Indies. Having no children of their own, the Estaughs adopted Elizabeth's nephew, Ebenezer Hopkins. The property which they bought for Hopkins's home is now the headquarters of the Camden County Cultural and Historical Commission.

QUAKER ROMANCE— LONGFELLOW VERSION

Unlikely as it may seem, the romance of Elizabeth Haddon and John Estaugh turned up as one of the stories in Henry Wadsworth Longfellow's *Tales of A Wayside Inn.* The poet certainly did not attribute to Elizabeth any of the traditional shyness of 18th century Quaker maidens.

Then it came to pass, one pleasant morning, that slowly
Up the road there came a cavalcade, as of pilgrims,
Men and women, wending their way to the Quarterly Meeting
In the neighboring town; and with them came riding John Estaugh.
At Elizabeth's door they stopped to rest, and alighting
Tasted the currant wine, and the bread of rye, and the honey
Brought from the hives, that stood by the sunny wall of the garden;
Then remounted their horses, refreshed, and continued their journey,
And Elizabeth with them, and Joseph, and Hannah the housemaid.
But, as they started, Elizabeth lingered a little, and leaning
Over her horse's neck, in a whisper said to John Estaugh:

"Tarry awhile behind, for I have something to tell thee,
Not to be spoken lightly, nor in the presence of others;
Them it concerneth not, only thee and me it concerneth."
And they rode slowly along through the woods, conversing together.
It was a pleasure to breathe the fragrant air of the forest;
It was a pleasure to live on that bright and happy May morning!

Then Elizabeth said, though still with a certain reluctance,
As if impelled to reveal a secret she fain would have guarded:
"I will no longer conceal what is laid upon me to tell thee;
I have received from the Lord a charge to love thee, John Estaugh."

BRINTON 1704 HOUSE

William Brinton put up this sturdy stone farmhouse in Birmingham Township, Pennsylvania in 1704. It underwent alterations and additions during the 250 years which followed, then was purchased by a Brinton. descendant and deeded to the Chester County Historical Society. Now, restored to its original form, it is maintained by the Brinton Family Association as an illustration of the life style of well-to-do Quakers who left England in Penn's time to live without persecution in country that had been wilderness shortly before.

Brinton was brought to Pennsylvania by his parents in 1684 when he was 14 years old. He married Jane Thatcher, daughter of a Quaker neighbor, in 1690. They lived in the parents' cabin until 1704 when there were six children and a desperate need for more space. Their new house was built on the same property, of stone quarried nearby. The walls are 22 inches thick. Most of the interior is panelled with walnut boards up to 22 inches wide. There are 27 windows with leaded sash in a diagonal pattern.

Inventories of the contents of the home were prepared for the estates of William and Jane Brinton and both have been preserved. Their house is furnished now with items of the type and period of the inventories. A few pieces are known to have belonged to the builder. Many others have come from Brinton family members, of whom there are now more than 900 in the United States.

The Brinton 1704 House is open to the public on a regular weekly schedule. It is on the old Wilmington-to-West-Chester road little more than a mile from the intersection of U.S. Highways 1 and 202.

Porches, gables and a large stone addition at the rear left the 1704 Brinton House looking like this in the 1880s. Restoration began by stripping the building down to its simple original form.

Birmingham Friends Meeting, organized in 1690, gathered at first in the Brinton cabin until a meeting house of cedar logs was erected in 1721. The present one of stone was built in 1763 a short distance north of the 1704 house. It was the scene of the 1980 reunion of the Brinton Family Association. Photograph by Theodore Brinton Hetzel.

SAMUEL POWEL(L) I, II AND III

William Penn never intended for Pennsylvania to become exclusively a Quaker province—and it didn't.

Penn's grant of religious freedom for people of all faiths from all nations was a guarantee that the Quakers eventually would be outnumbered, and they were. But there was another factor, too. Not all of the early Quaker families remained Quaker. The Powel family is a well-known example.

SAMUEL POWELL, I

The first Samuel Powell was a Quaker orphan brought to Philadelphia by his aunt. She married the Quaker carpenter, John Parsons, and young Samuel grew up in their household. He learned the carpenter's trade and inherited Parson's "work tools and instruments". Parson's will also provided a cash legacy for Powell, but only if he chose for his bride a Quaker girl who met "the approbation and assent" of his aunt and "the consent of Friends".

Samuel more than qualified for the legacy by marrying Abigail Wilcox, a member of a family in good standing with the Meeting. Their wedding was such an outstanding affair among Friends that William and Hannah Penn were in attendance as was Edward Shippen, the Quaker Mayor of the city.

Samuel Powell prospered at his trade and was widely known in Philadelphia as "the rich carpenter".

SAMUEL POWEL, II

Samuel's son, the second Samuel, born in 1705, altered the spelling of his family name by dropping the final letter "l". He went into the mercantile business and earned a vast fortune. He was an active member of Friends Meeting and married Mary Morris, daughter of the substantial Quaker brewer, Anthony Morris.

Samuel, II, died at the age of 42. He owned the entire block of Pine Street between Front and Second. In his will he left a lot in that block to the Philadelphia Monthly Meeting "if the members shall agree to build a meeting house there." This was on Society Hill, a section of the city then becoming well settled. The Meeting accepted the land gladly.

For a century or more the Pine Street Meeting, also known as the Hill Meeting, was a reminder to Friends, of their solid member, Samuel Powel, II.

SAMUEL POWEL, III

The third Samuel, a birthright Friend born in 1738, inherited two large fortunes—his father's and his grandfather's—while still a student in the second class of the new College of Philadelphia. Upon graduation at age 21 he found in his possession some ninety houses in Philadelphia and a fine country place across the river in New Jersey.

For most of a year, Powel joined in the activities of a group of young Quakers who called themselves "The Society Meeting Weekly in the City of Philadelphia for Their Mutual Improvement in Useful Knowledge". In 1760, however, he departed for Europe for the Grand Tour then fashionable among young gentlemen of wealth and family background. He did not return home for seven years.

Powel found other young Philadelphians of similar circumstance in London, among them John Morgan, William Shippen and William Logan. He helped support the promising young painter, Benjamin West. He traveled widely and enjoyed the company of the most fashionable society both in England and on the continent. He was presented to the King in London and to the Pope in Rome. He traveled for weeks at a time as the companion of the Duke of York.

Midway during Powel's life abroad, the Anglican clergyman William Smith, provost of the College of Philadelphia, was in London when the young man was presented at court. "I almost got him (Powel) dubbed a knight," Smith wrote later, "but we thought it would be idle and considered a design to separate him from his old Friends, the Quakers of Philadelphia."

Before he returned home, Powel wrote to his friend, the Reverend Richard Peters, of Philadelphia, that he wanted to be baptized in the Anglican Church, and soon after he arrived in Philadelphia he became a communicant and pew holder at Saint Peters Church which had been erected during his absence at Third and Pine Streets in the Society Hill section.

Samuel Powel, III married Elizabeth Willing, daughter of the financier Thomas Willing, whose fortune was equal to or greater than Powel's. They took up residence in the stately townhouse at 244 South Third Street now perhaps the best of Philadelphia's restored colonial townhouses. The house was a center for the social life of wealthy Philadelphians. George and Martha Washington were regularly entertained there, and the Powels were guests at Mount Vernon.

The large section of Philadelphia now called Powelton retains the name of the family's country place west of the Schuylkill.

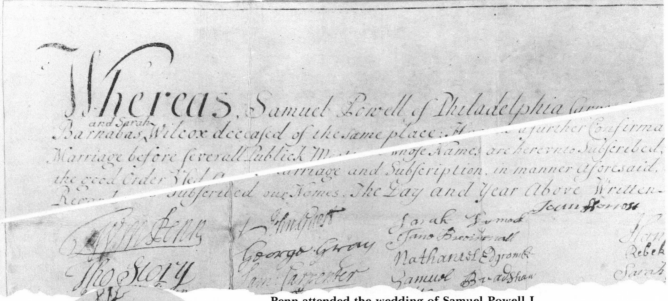

Whereas Samuel Powell *of Philadelphia* and Sarah *Barnabas Wilcox deceased of the same place...*

Penn attended the wedding of Samuel Powell I.

Old Hill Meeting House. Photo made just before demolition 1861.

Samuel Powel, III and his town house as it looks today.

A GENTLEMAN OF UNIVERSAL LEARNING

James Logan.
As a young man, he aided Penn; in later years he advised Benjamin Franklin.

The young man who came to Pennsylvania in 1699 as the Governor's secretary became one of the truly notable figures in the history of the province.

Remaining behind when Penn returned permanently to England, James Logan was for fifty years the administrator, confidential agent and personal friend of the Penn family. He was probably the most influential person in Pennsylvania and, at the same time, a remarkably well-rounded man—an able executive, a successful business man, a trusted friend of the Indians, a scientist, a linguist and a bibliophile without equal in colonial America.

In Philadelphia today, Logan's career is not well known, but his name is a familiar one. A section of northwest Philadelphia is called Logan, as are a Post Office, a school, a railroad station, a street, a number of business houses, and the well-kept square which divides the Parkway at 19th Street.

Stenton Mansion, the home James Logan built in 1728 in the midst of 500 acres of woodland, is still in existence, owned by the city and open to visitors just a short distance from the busy intersection of Broad Street and Roosevelt Boulevard.

James Logan's mansion "Stenton" still bears the imprint of the man who built it and made it his home.

Born in Ireland, the son of a Scotch Quaker schoolmaster, Logan learned early in life to teach himself almost anything from a book. He had mastered some Latin, Greek and Hebrew before he was 13. Later he learned French and Spanish. He was accomplished in mathematics. He became a schoolmaster in England at age 19 and then, hoping to become wealthy, he undertook a career as a linen merchant. His failure in that left him ready to accept William Penn's invitation to accompany him to America.

Logan's passion was books. He corresponded at length with the booksellers of Europe, collected the finest library on this side of the Atlantic, and left it to the people of Philadelphia. He provided a small library building on Sixth Street "behind the State House" to contain his books and directed that they should be available for scholars without cost. Most of his collection is still intact, more than 2000 volumes, most of them on scientific or philosophical subjects and many of them in Latin, Greek or Hebrew.

The "Loganian Library" is now administered by the Library Company of Philadelphia, founded in 1731 by Benjamin Franklin. When Franklin and his group of young apprentices were organizing their library, they appealed to Logan, then 30 years older, to help in the selection of their books because he was "a gentleman of universal learning, and the best judge of books in these parts."

Logan Square on Philadelphia's Franklin Parkway; in the background, City Hall with the statue of William Penn overlooking his city.

"THEE WAS WILLING ENOUGH . . ."

Unlike many Quakers, James Logan did not oppose defensive warfare.

When attack on the English colonies was feared during war with France, Logan aided Franklin finance purchase of cannon for a battery along the Delaware.

Logan told Franklin about the trans-Atlantic voyage with Penn in 1699. Franklin repeated it in his *Autobiography*:

"It was war-time and their ship was chas'd by an armed vessel, suppos'd to be an enemy. Their captain prepared for defense but told William Penn, and his company of Quakers that he did not expect their assistance and they might retire into the cabin, which they did except James Logan who chose to stay upon deck and was quarter'd to a gun.

"The suppos'd enemy prov'd a friend, so there was no fighting; but when the secretary went down to communicate the intelligence, William Penn rebuk'd him severely for staying upon deck and undertaking to assist in defending the vessel, contrary to the principles of Friends, especially as it had not been required by the captain.

"This reproof being before all the company piqu'd the secretary, who answer'd:

"'I being thy servant, why did thee not order me to come down? But thee was willing enough that I should stay and help to fight the ship when thee thought there was danger.'"

PRIMITIVE HALL—JOSEPH & MARY LEVIS PENNOCK

Primitive Hall, built in 1738.

Joseph
Pennock
(1677—1771).

PRIMITIVE HALL FOUNDATION

Joseph and Mary Levis Pennock built this fine manor house in Chester County in 1738. It is still owned and maintained by some of their descendants who formed the Primitive Hall Foundation.

Facing south on a still-quiet and restful hill on Pennsylvania Route 841 South of Coatesville, the roomy brick house was designed for large families and was on occasion occupied by two generations of Pennocks. A wide center hall runs through from front to back. A well-proportioned open stairwell rises in the center all the way from first floor to attic. Four large rooms with corner fire-places share one chimney on the east, another four, one on the west. Most of the woodwork is original.

• • •

Joseph Pennock, born in Ireland in 1677, inherited more than 5000 acres of Pennsylvania land from his wealthy Quaker grandfather when he was about 20. He came to America in 1701, settling first in Philadelphia and marrying Mary Levis in 1705. She was the daughter of a family which came from England in 1682, early members of Darby Friends Meeting. Her father, Samuel Levis was a member of William Penn's Council and later an Assemblyman. He operated a paper mill on Darby Creek.

Joseph and Mary Pennock moved to Chester County in 1710 and in 1738 built Primitive Hall, the ancestral home of so many Pennock and other families in Pennsylvania and throughout the nation.

Although a birthright Friend, Joseph Pennock as a young man in Philadelphia was not always "in unity" with the Society, but after moving to the country he apparently changed his ways, as evidenced by this minute of the monthly meeting:

> "Joseph Pennock offered a paper condemning his outgoing in time past from Truth and Friends, and signifying his desire to come nearer to Friends, which this meeting accepts of."

Pennock became a long-time member of the Pennsylvania Assembly, a Justice of the Peace and an important figure in the province. He died in 1771.

THE SHIPLEYS AND "WILLINGTOWN"

About twenty years after Mary Levis married Joseph Pennock, her younger sister, Elizabeth, married William Shipley, a widower, of Ridley, Pennsylvania.

As a minister of the Society of Friends, Elizabeth frequently made long horseback journeys to other provinces on religious missions. One spring day in 1735, en route to Maryland on such a journey, she was greatly affected by the prospect from the top of a steep hill in a wooded area near the Delaware River. She felt it was exactly the place she had seen in a dream—a place where the Lord wanted her and her husband to settle for the future benefit of Friends and the community.

William Shipley visited the tiny Quaker settlement of Willingtown which had sprung up nearby the year before. He bought land and began construction of a house at Fourth Street and another thoroughfare which is still called Shipley Street. Shipley transferred his business to Willingtown. After the family moved in the Shipley home was the gathering place for what eventually became Wilmington Friends Meeting. The first meeting house was built on land donated by the Shipleys at Fourth and West Streets in 1738.

As Willingtown grew into the city of Wilmington, a larger meeting house was erected across West Street at the same intersection, an unusual building for a meeting house, square in shape and two stories high topped with a cupola. It served until 1817 when Friends began using the large brick meeting house which was built on the same site. The Meeting still worships there today.

The Shipley House, Wilmington, where Friends meetings were held before 1738.

Second meeting house, Wilmington, Fourth and West Streets.

Present Wilmington Meeting House, built 1817.

BENJAMIN LAY, QUAKER PROTESTER

An intense little man, 55 inches tall with humped back, spindly legs and a flowing white beard haunted Philadelphia for twenty-five years with colorful and dramatic protests against slavery. He was Benjamin Lay, English Quaker, who arrived in

QUAKER COLLECTION, HAVERFORD COLLEGE LIBRARY

the city at the age of 54 after years of witnessing the slave trade first hand as a common seaman.

Soon after reaching Philadelphia, Lay engaged Benjamin Franklin to print a vitriolic booklet, *All Slave-keepers, Apostates* which denounced all who kept slaves, and especially those professing membership in Friends Meetings. His words were so bitter, the public so disturbed, that Philadelphia Monthy Meeting directed the Clerk to publish a newspaper announcement that Lay did not speak for the Meeting. Yet before Lay's death, the Meeting revised its discipline to disown any who continued to be slave-holders.

Lay once attended Yearly Meeting at Burlington concealing under his long coat a pig bladder filled with red berry juice. While speaking, he appeared to stab himself with a small knife, sending the blood-like liquid spurting out—demonstrating, he said, the bloody deeds of the slave trade.

He stood on a cold First Day morning outside Abington Meeting with one foot bare in the snow. He denounced all who expressed any concern. "You pretend compassion for me, yet do not feel for the slaves who are half-clad."

Once he kidnapped the child of a slave-holding neighbor, keeping the youngster all day to teach the parents the anguish of separated slave families.

Lay was a vegetarian and opposed to the use of tea or tobacco. He sometimes carried smokers' pipes into meetings for worship and broke them there dramatically. On one occasion he drew a large crowd in the public market by smashing china tea cups against the paving stones.

Lay built a stone cottage on a small farm, giving rise to a popular impression that he lived in a cave. In later years he boarded at the farm of John Phipps, a member of Abington Meeting. He was buried in the graveyard beside the Meeting house.

The print reproduced here was certainly not intended to be flattering to Benjamin Lay. Yet the publisher felt in honesty he had to attach this note to it:

> "Benjamin Lay lived to the age of 80, in the latter part of which he observed extreme temperance in his eating and drinking. His fondness for peculiarity in dress and customs sometimes subjected him to the ridicule of the ignorant, but his friends who were intimate with him thought him an honest, religious man."

32

THE QUAKER BOTANISTS—I

JOHN BARTRAM AND HUMPHREY MARSHALL

Philadelphia Yearly Meeting produced a surprising number of self-educated Quaker farmers who became masters in the science of botany.

The first were John Bartram, of Philadelphia, and his younger cousin, Humphrey Marshall, of Chester County. They were grandsons of James Hunt, an English Friend and widower who brought his two daughters to Pennsylvania in 1684.

• • •

John Bartram, born in 1699, studied plants as a farm boy and eventually made his living by traveling the east coast collecting seeds and seedlings for his own nursery and for owners of estates in England. Aided by James Logan and Benjamin Franklin, he corresponded with scientists abroad and became well-known in Europe. His son, William, travelled with him and made botanical drawings for the British Museum.

After his second marriage to Ann Mendinhall, of Concord Meeting, in 1729, Bartram built a sturdy dwelling of large hand-hewn stones on the Schuylkill just below Grays Ferry. His garden and arboretum sloped down from the house to the river. The property is now owned by the City of Philadelphia and maintained as a public park. The John Bartram Association, which includes some of his descendants, provided appropriate furniture and helps with maintenance.

• • •

Humphrey Marshall, born in 1722, had little formal education and was apprenticed to a stone mason. Nevertheless, influenced, no doubt, by his older cousin, he obtained books, studied plants and their reproduction and began collections of his own. He, too, sold specimens to wealthy Europeans. In 1785 he published the first American book on botany, an alphabetical catalogue of native trees and shrubs.

Humphrey Marshall was one of the members of the Committee for Westtown Boarding School and did the first pruning of the orchard on the school's farm. Both Marshall and Bartram were elected members of the American Philosophical Society in recognition of their scientific accomplishments.

CAROLINE BARTRAM GIBSON

Bartram Family Reunion—1893—on the occasion of the ancestral home becoming a permanent memorial to the man who built it in 1729.

WISTARS AND WISTERS

Two brothers named Wüster came to Philadelphia from Germany ten years apart. When Caspar, the elder, arrived in 1717, his last name was Anglicized to Wistar. But when John came along in 1727, his name was spelled Wister. Each family retained its own spelling, to the confusion of genealogists and historians ever since.

The brother called Wistar started as apprentice to a button-maker and advanced to be a successful manufacturer. He married a Germantown girl at Germantown Friends Meeting in 1726. Later he purchased extensive land holdings in South Jersey, established one of America's earliest glassworks and founded the town of Wistarburg. He brought workmen from Europe to teach him and his son the secrets of glass-making. A few old homes and Friends meeting houses near Salem still have panes of Wistarburg glass. The greenish glassware turned out in Wistar's factory is now displayed in museums.

Dr. Caspar Wistar, grandson and namesake of the first Caspar, became one of Philadelphia's many great Quaker physicians. Another descendant, General Isaac J. Wistar founded Wistar Institute of Anatomy and Science in Philadelphia.

A friend of Dr. Caspar Wistar named a beautiful flowering vine after him—and this is a reminder that its correct spelling is wist*aria*, not wist*eria*.

• • •

The brother called Wister began as a grower of fruits and grapes and in time earned a fortune as a Philadelphia wine merchant. He was one of the city's first prosperous Quakers to build a summer residence in the village of Germantown.

John Wister sent his family to the country estate of a distant relative, the widow Hannah Foulke, in North Wales when British capture of Philadelphia was threatened. Washington's American army was in control of that territory and the Foulke mansion became headquarters for General William Smallwood, of Maryland. John Wister's grand-daughter, Sally, kept a chatty teen-ager's diary of her stay there for the benefit of Debbie Norris, her classmate at Anthony Benezet's school.

Sally's journal is full of excitement and fun in the company of young officers of Smallwood's staff. But back in the city, Grandfather John was the dismal host of officers on the British side:

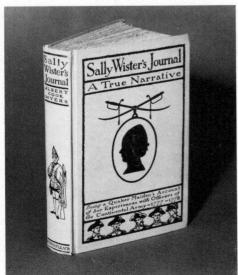

> *"They have taken the best rooms in the house and I must live in the back building. Oh, it most kills me to be so ill-treated in my old age, that I must leave my bedchamber where I have lodged near 30 years to a stranger."*

WYCK—HOME OF NINE QUAKER GENERATIONS

Wyck is a delightful mini-plantation in the heart of modern Germantown at Walnut Lane and Germantown Avenue—complete with an historic house, 2½ acres of carefully-tended grounds, a formal, box-bordered rose garden, carriage house, smokehouse and icehouse. Nine generations of one Quaker family lived there from 1690 until 1973.

Hans Milan, a German Friend, built the first small stone house on the property. Later he put up a second similar little dwelling directly in front of it for his daughter, and the two sections were united sometime before the Revolution. Caspar Wistar became one of the owners when he married Katherine Jansen, a granddaughter of Wyck's builder. They in turn passed the place to their daughter, Margaret and her husband, Reuben Haines. Thereafter Wyck was owned and occupied by nine generations of the family until deeded, together with its furnishings and tens of thousands of family documents, to the Wyck Charitable Trust for the benefit of the public.

Wyck is now owned and maintained by the trustees, including some family members of the tenth generation. It is open as a museum of Quaker lifestyle over nearly three centuries. The family papers are being catalogued for study by Quaker historians.

Wyck—Then and Now.   THE WYCK CHARITABLE TRUST

GRUMBLETHORPE AND WISTER'S WOODS

The summer residence built by John Wister in 1740 has also survived. Called Grumblethorpe, it stands close to the sidewalk of Germantown Avenue directly opposite Indian Queen Lane. Behind it stretches a deep expanse of yard, garden and woodland still known in Germantown as Wister's Woods. The oak timbers for the solid house were cut on the property, and the stone was quarried close by.

While unoccupied by the Wister family, Grumblethorpe was taken over by British General James Agnew in late September, 1777. He was killed a week later in the Battle of Germantown.

After the war, the old house was converted for year-round use and descended from generation to generation until transferred to the Philadelphia Society for the Preservation of Landmarks founded by Frances A. Wister in 1931. Guides provide tours at scheduled times.

Grumblethorpe.

PHILADELPHIA SOCIETY FOR THE PRESERVATION OF LANDMARKS

NOTES FOR THE TERCENTENARY

1. MEETINGS FOR BUSINESS—1676

Since the beginning, Friends have distinguished between gatherings held weekly for religious worship and monthly meetings to conduct the business affairs of the Society. Meetings for business deal with such matters as property management, aid for the "necessitous", admissions to membership, and marriages. Quite frequently, especially in the old days, monthly meetings gave weighty consideration to the disciplining of members "who walk disorderly."

> *"At a meeting the last day of the fifth month, 1676, it was unanimously consented unto that the first second day of the week (Monday) in every month the Friends within the town of New Salem, in Fenwick Colony and all Friends belonging thereunto, do monthly meet together, to consider of outward business, and of such as have been convinced and walk disorderly, that they may with all gravity and uprightness to God and in tenderness of spirit and love to their souls be admonished, exhorted and also reproved . . . ."*

2. PETTICOATS, SNUFF AND FANS—1726

From an epistle of Women's Yearly Meeting:

> *"We are willing in the pure love of Truth . . . tenderly to caution and advise our Friends against these things which we think inconsistent with our ancient Christian testimony of plainness in apparel, etc.*
>
> *"First, that immodest fashion of hooped petticoats . . .*
>
> *"Likewise that all Friends be careful to avoid superfluity of furniture in their houses and, as much as may be, to refrain using gaudy flowered or striped callicos and stuffs.*
>
> *"Also, that no Friends use that irreverent practice of taking snuff or handing snuff-boxes one to another in Meetings.*
>
> *"Also, that Friends avoid the unnecessary use of fans in Meetings lest it divert the mind from the more inward and spiritual exercise which all ought to be concerned in . . ."*

3. PAID POLITICAL ANNOUNCEMENT—1744

Newspaper ad placed by Quaker Nicholas Scull, candidate for re-election as Philadelphia Sheriff:

> *"Though it has not till this time been customary to request your votes in print, yet, that method being now introduced, I think myself obliged in this public manner to return to you my hearty thanks for the favors I have already received, and to acquaint you that I intend again to stand a candidate for the Sheriff's office, and request your interest at the next election to favor your real friend."*

FRANKLIN AND THE QUAKERS

It was most appropriate that the first day Benjamin Franklin spent in Philadelphia at the age of 17, he found himself in the Great Meeting House at a Quaker meeting for worship.

Franklin was not a Friend (nor member of any other organized religious group) but throughout his long life he was closely associated with Quakers and was aided by them in both his business and his public life.

In his *Autobiography* Franklin tells how he left Boston to look for work in New York, failed, then walked for two days across New Jersey to Burlington. He rowed all night to pay his passage down the Delaware River and reached Philadelphia tired and hungry on a Sunday morning. After walking a short distance near the waterfront, he purchased "three great, puffy rolls":

> *"Thus refreshed, I walked again up the street, which by this time had many clean-dressed people in it, who were all walking the same way. I joined them, and thereby was led to the Great Meeting House of the Quakers near the market. (Second and High Streets).*

> *"I sat down among them and, after looking around a while and hearing nothing said, being very drowsy thro' labor and want of rest the preceding night, I fell fast asleep, and continu'd so till the meeting broke up, when one was kind enough to rouse me."*

FRANKLIN'S QUAKER FRIENDS

Pennsylvania Hospital—1755.

Most Philadelphians know the part Benjamin Franklin played in founding numerous organizations and institutions which are thriving in the City of Philadelphia today. Not generally remembered, however, is the extent to which Philadelphia Quakers supported Franklin and contributed to the success of his ventures.

Pennsylvania Hospital in Philadelphia, the first such institution in the country, was originally proposed by Dr. Thomas Bond. Franklin is regarded as co-founder because he conceived the fund-raising steps which made the hospital possible. Quakers provided most of the private money, and the Quaker majority in the Assembly voted the public funds for it.

For years, Pennsylvania was called "The Quaker Hospital". Joshua Crosby, Quaker merchant, was the first President. John Reynell, another Friend, was first Treasurer. A majority of the members of the original Board of Managers belonged to Friends meetings. Reynell's nephew, Samuel Coates, served fifty years as a Manager of the institution, part of that time as its President. Mordecai Lewis, still another Quaker business man, was elected Treasurer in 1780 and members of his family succeeded him in that office for more than a hundred years.

Pennsylvania Hospital opened a Department for the Insane on a 100-acre farm in West Philadelphia in 1841, its grounds and two large buildings surrounded by a high stone wall. Generations of Philadelphians knew this institution as "Kirkbrides" rather than as a unit of the downtown hospital. Thomas Story Kirkbride was a Quaker physician who received his training at Friends Hospital and at age 31 was made Physician-in-Chief and Superintendent of the new department. He served in that capacity until his death some forty years later, achieving a national reputation for advances in care of the mentally ill.

THE LIBRARY COMPANY (1731)—Nearly half of the shareholders in Franklin's first public undertaking, the Library Company of Philadelphia, were Quakers, and four were on the first Board of Managers. The minute book notes their objections when a petition to the Governor was not couched in the plain language used to address everyone else.

AMERICAN PHILOSOPHICAL SOCIETY (1743) Five of Franklin's Quaker associates comprised a majority of the first Board of Directors.

PHILADELPHIA CONTRIBUTIONSHIP FOR INSURANCE OF HOUSES FROM LOSS BY FIRE (1752)—Nine of the twelve members of the original Board of Franklin's fire insurance company were Friends in good standing with the Philadelphia Meeting, and a tenth had only just been disowned for marrying "out of meeting". Joseph Saunders, Quaker merchant, was the first Clerk, or chief executive.

First home of the Library Company.

THOMAS DENHAM

Thomas Denham, a Philadelphia merchant, was young Franklin's first Quaker benefactor.

Franklin's skill as a printer was so great at age 19 that he attracted the attention of Pennsylvania's Governor, Sir William Keith. Trouble was, Keith was an irresponsible busybody addicted to making big promises. The inexperienced Franklin took off for London to buy type and other supplies, believing that Keith would set him up in business and make him official government printer. But the Governor never even wrote the letters of introduction he had promised. Franklin was stranded in London but fortunately competent enough to find work in print shops there.

Denham was a passenger on the ship which carried Franklin across the Atlantic. He became interested in the young man and kept in touch with him in London. When ready to return to Philadelphia, Denham offered to pay Franklin's passage and to give him a job in his store back home. After a year and a half of knocking about on his own, Franklin was glad to accept.

Franklin might have given up printing and become a merchant, for he learned quickly under Denham's guidance.

"I attended the business diligently, studied accounts and grew, in a little time, expert at selling. We lodg'd and boarded together; he counseled me as a father . . ."

But Denham died within a few months, leaving a will which cancelled the debts Franklin still owed for cash advances in excess of wages. Benjamin Franklin went back to work in the print shop of Samuel Keimer.

JOSEPH BREINTNAL

Joseph Breintnal, a writer, copier of deeds and active member of Philadelphia Monthly Meeting, brought the first important piece of business to Franklin and his young partner, Hugh Meredith, when the two went into business for themselves in 1728.

Philadelphia Meeting had wanted for several years to get out a printing of Sewel's *History of the Rise, Increase and Progress of the Christian People Called Quakers*, but Keimer's shop had long delayed it. Breintnal arranged for Franklin's shop to help finish it.

THE AUTOBIOGRAPHY

Had it not been for Franklin's friend, Abel James, a Quaker merchant in Philadelphia, *The Autobiography of Benjamin Franklin* might never have become a classic in American school rooms.

Franklin began writing the story of his life in the form of a letter to his son, not intending it for publication. He covered only the first 25 years. Then the manuscript was lost sight of until Abel James in 1783 found it in papers he was reviewing as executor of an estate. He sent it to Franklin, who was then in Paris, urging him to continue the story.

Franklin sent the manuscript to a friend in France, who agreed with James, whereupon Franklin resumed his story, this time anticipating its publication. Unfortunately, he never finished it beyond the events of 1757 and so did not cover the important historical years of his life.

Franklin died in 1790. The first edition of the autobiography was published in French in Paris in 1791, a testimony to the admiration in which Franklin was held by the people of France.

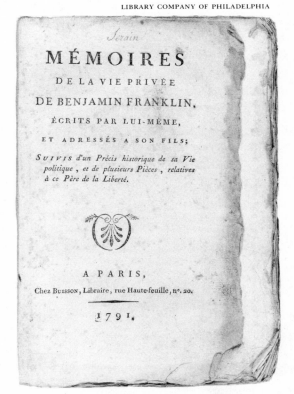

MÉMOIRES
DE LA VIE PRIVÉE
DE BENJAMIN FRANKLIN,
ÉCRITS PAR LUI-MÊME,
ET ADRESSÉS A SON FILS;
SUIVIS d'un Précis historique de sa Vie politique, et de plusieurs Pièces, relatives à ce Père de la Liberté.

A PARIS,
Chez BUISSON, Libraire, rue Haute-feuille, n°. 20.
1791.

Franklin's Autobiography—First Edition.

THE STATE HOUSE BELL

Since Philadelphia was the capital of Pennsylvania, the Assembly in 1732 ordered construction of a large public building to house the government. At first, the State House had no tower, but in 1751—an important anniversary in William Penn's province—it was decided to erect one and purchase a bell for it.

The occasion was the fiftieth anniversary of Penn's Charter of Liberties of 1701. Quaker Speaker Isaac Norris was head of the committee responsible for the bell. Seeking an inscription for it, he found a most appropriate verse in the Biblical Book of Leviticus: "And ye shall hallow the fiftieth year, and proclaim liberty throughout all the land unto all the inhabitants thereof; it shall be a jubilee unto you . . ."

Norris promptly got off a letter to the provincial agent in London. A copy can still be seen in the Norris letterbook at the Historical Society of Pennsylvania.

> *"Get us a good bell of about two thousand pounds weight . . .*
>
> *"Let the bell be cast by the best workmen and examined carefully before it is shipped with the following words well shaped in large letters round it:*
>
> *"By order of the Assembly of the Province of Pennsylvania for the State House in the City of Philada, 1752, and underneath:*
>
> *"Proclaim Liberty 'thro all the land to all the inhabitants thereof—Levit. XXV 10'"*

The great bell had to be recast in Philadelphia by "two ingenious workmen" Pass and Stowe. It was 1753 before it could be raised to the new State House tower. For 23 years it hung there to honor William Penn and the liberty he granted his Pennsylvania settlers.

In 1776 the State House bell became a symbol of liberty for all Americans.

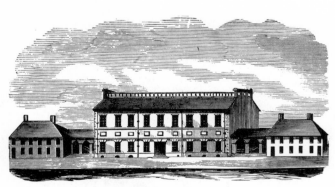

The State House before 1751.

The bell tower ordered in 1751 to commemorate Penn's Charter of Liberties.

PENN'S "SEED OF A NATION"

After the Declaration of Independence, the Pennsylvania State House became headquarters for the American Revolution. This is where the Continental Congress met to direct the war. When peace was restored, this is where the United States of America was formed by the Constitutional Convention of 1787. While the city of Washington was being built, Philadelphia was the capital of the new nation.

How much of all this had William Penn forseen?

In a letter written within a day or so after the King approved the charter for Pennsylvania, in 1681, Penn wrote:

"Thou mayest communicate my grant to friends, and expect shortly my proposals.

"'Tis a clear and just thing, and my God that has given it me through many difficulties will, I believe, bless and make it the seed of a nation. . ."

"QUAKER SAINTS"

Philadelphia Yearly Meeting produced in colonial days two men whose extraordinary dedication to "Truth" and human brotherhood resulted in each of them being characterized on numerous occasions as "a Quaker Saint". Anthony Benezet was one, John Woolman the other.

ANTHONY BENEZET

Benezet, born in France, apprenticed to a Quaker in London and convinced as a Friend there, came to Philadelphia with his family at the age of 18 in 1731. For a while he tried business with his well-to-do brothers, but he gave it up to become a teacher and dedicate 40 years of his life to the service of humanity. He became a leader in the education of women and of poor blacks. He crusaded tirelessly against slavery and cultivated friendship with the Indians. He regarded himself as a teacher rather than a preacher, and he was at times critical of ministers who, he said "live delicately and wear soft raiment."

Benezet was a prolific writer, particularly in attacking the slave trade. His *Epistle of Caution and Advice Concerning the Importation and Purchase of Slaves* demanded that members of the Society of Friends abandon slave-holding. Some of his publications were distributed in England as well as in the colonies, and eventually he campaigned against slavery throughout the British empire. He was one of the leaders who succeeded in having Philadelphia Meeting adopt a minute of censure and disownment for Friends who persisted in slave-keeping.

When Great Britain drove French-speaking Acadians from Nova Scotia at the start of the French and Indian War, Benezet almost singlehandedly undertook to care for 450 of the impoverished Acadian exiles who were sent to Philadelphia. Neither City nor Province wanted responsibility for helping the Acadians, so Benezet had himself designated agent to assist them. He raised money, provided food, and nursed the sick. He persuaded a Friend, Samuel Emlen, to donate ground on Pine Street near Fifth and built small cottages to house the exiles.

Employed first at the Friends Public School, Benezet left to open a new institution which would provide secondary schooling for girls. For twenty years he maintained a night school for black children in his own home at his own expense, finally persuading the Meeting to sponsor the project and to open a black school in Willings Alley which Benezet taught during his last years. When he died in 1784 he left a trust fund for the education of blacks. It is still administered for that purpose by the Friends Education Committee.

Anthony Benezet's House
First Home of the Philadelphia Yearly Meeting Library. Benezet ran a night school here for poor black children.

Anthony Benezet's schoolmaster's desk, now owned by Philadelphia Monthly Meeting.

JOHN WOOLMAN

One of a family of 13 children, John Woolman was born in 1720 on a farm on Rancocas Creek in New Jersey. At an early age he moved into nearby Mount Holly to take up shop-keeping. He was successful, but gave up trade when he found that too much money-making interfered with his intense spiritual life. Thereafter he worked as a tailor and devoted most of his life to religious concerns. He became a Friends minister in his twenties and at 26 began traveling ministry into other provinces.

Within the Yearly Meeting, John Woodman became a close friend of Anthony Benezet and the two worked tirelessly together in opposing slavery—particularly slave-keeping by members of the Society. He attracted much notice with his *Some Considerations on the Keeping of Negroes*. He wrote pamphlets, letters and books which were widely circulated in America and in England. In 1758, the Meeting made him head of the committee sent to interview all Friends who still held slaves and try to convince them to desist.

Woolman sought to divorce himself from all contact with slavery and the slave trade. He declined to be a guest in houses where he would be served by slaves. He stopped using sugar and molasses and other West Indian products "on account of the hard use of the slaves who raised it." During his late years he wore white or natural-color clothing to protest the use of dyes from slave countries.

During the warfare with the French and their Indian allies, Woolman made a long pilgrimage by foot into dangerous Indian country along the Susquehanna River in Pennsylvania "in order to spend some time with Indians, that I might feel and understand their life and the spirit they live in."

Woolman's last religious mission was to England in 1772. Although able to afford better, he insisted on traveling in the steerage throughout a 39-day Atlantic crossing. "It hath afforded me sundry opportunities of seeing, hearing and feeling with respect to the life and spirit of many poor sailors", he wrote. He reached London just in time for Yearly Meeting, then departed for an arduous three-month trek on foot to visit quarterly and monthly meetings.

At York, Woolman was stricken with smallpox and died within two weeks at the residence of one of the elders of York Meeting. He was buried in the graveyard of the Friends Meeting at York.

WOOLMAN'S JOURNAL

For fifteen years, John Woolman kept a detailed journal of his religious visits and his inner spiritual experiences. Just before his departure for England in 1772 he edited his writing as far as he had gone, and left the journal in the care of John Pemberton, Clerk of the Committee for Sufferings (the interim authority between Yearly Meetings.) He directed its publication "if it should please the Lord to remove me from this stage of life before I return."

After news of his death reached Philadelphia, a committee including Anthony Benezet edited and published the Woolman Journal. The first edition appeared in 1774.

John Woolman built this house in Mount Holly, N.J. as a wedding present for his daughter in 1771. It now serves as a museum.

John Woolman
A drawing made by one of Woolman's
friends after Woolman's death.

BY THE HONOURABLE
R O B E R T H U N T E R M O R R I S, Efq;

Lieutenant Governor, and Commander in Chief of the Province of *Pennfylvania*, and Counties of *New-Caftle*, *Kent* and *Suffex*, upon *Delaware*,

A PROCLAMATION.

WHEREAS the *Delaware* Tribe of *Indians*, and others, in Confederacy with them, have, for fome Time paft, without the leaft Provocation, and contrary to their moft folemn Treaties, fallen upon this Province, and in a moft cruel, favage and perfidious Manner, killed and butchered great Numbers of the Inhabitants, and carried others into barbarous Captivity, burning and deftroying their Habitations, and laying wafte the Country: AND WHEREAS, notwithftanding the friendly Remonftrances made to them by this Government, and the Interpofition and pofitive Orders of our faithful Friends and Allies the *Six Nations*, to whom they owe Obedience and Subjection, requiring and commanding them to defift from any further Acts of Hoftility againft us, and to return to their Allegiance, the faid *Indians* do ftill continue their cruel Murders and Ravages, fparing neither Age nor Sex: I HAVE THEREFORE, by and with the Advice and Confent of the Council, thought fit to iffue this Proclamation; and do hereby declare the faid *Delaware Indians*, and all others, who, in Conjunction with them, have committed Hoftilities againft His Majefty's Subjects within this Province, to be Enemies, Rebels and Traitors to His Moft Sacred Majefty. AND I do hereby requi... all H... ... Sub... ... his Prov... ... hofe of ...

INDIAN WAR IN PENNSYLVANIA

Penn's heirs and successors not only drew away from the Society of Friends but also abandoned his principles of fair dealing with the Indians. The Delawares, original inhabitants of Pennsylvania, were cheated in the infamous "Walking Purchase" of 1737 and again in 1754 when the province "bought" from the Iroquois Indians in New York vast stretches of territory that had been homeland of the Delawares. The defrauded red men became allies of the French and raided a number of western Pennsylvania settlements.

In 1756 Pennsylvania's Governor Robert Morris declared war on the Delawares and issued this proclamation describing them as "enemies, rebels and traitors". He offered bounties not only for prisoners but also for the scalps of Delaware Indians, male and female.

The Quakers who controlled the Assembly were in an impossible position. They did not support war and were unwilling to appropriate funds for defense of the frontier. The great majority of Friends located in Philadelphia and near it were accused of sacrificing the lives of non-Quakers to the west. London Yearly Meeting sent two emissaries to Pennsylvania to offer counsel. The result was some Quaker Assemblymen resigned or declined to stand for re-election. Control of Pennsyl-

vania's legislature passed into the hands of non-Quakers.

When Pennsylvania troops under Colonel Armstrong wiped out the Indian village of Kittanning in reprisal for raids on white settlers, Philadelphia City Council ordered silver medals for all the officers. Quakers formed the Friendly Association for Regaining and Preserving Peace with the Indians. They ordered silver medals and other trinkets to give to Indians as gestures of peace. Both the war medals and the peace medals were made by Quaker silversmith, Joseph Richardson.

THE PAXTON BOYS

Philadelphia was thrown into a panic in 1764 when an armed mob named "The Paxton Boys" was reported marching on the city to massacre a group of Indians who had taken refuge within it. The Paxtons had murdered a score of peaceful Indian basket-weavers in Lancaster County the year before.

The evil reputation of the Paxtons brought out armed citizens who joined the militia in preparing for defense. Many young Quakers were among them. The Friends Meeting House was used as a temporary barracks and guns were stored in the gallery.

Benjamin Franklin led a delegation to meet the desperadoes, who gave up and quietly dispersed when they realized they faced armed resistance. Not a shot was fired. Afterwards, the incident was ridiculed and much fun poked at the Quakers who had sprung to arms. This early political cartoon showed soldiers lined up with cannon to defend the Courthouse and the Meeting House at Second and Market Streets.

Come all ye Brave Delphia's, and Listen to Me.
A Story of Truth, I'll unfold unto thee
'Tis of the Paxtonians, as You shall Hear:
Who Caused this City in Arms to appear.

Brave P——n then Assembled his Council with Speed.
The Inhabitants too, for there Ne'er was more need
To Go to the State House, and there to Attend.
With all the Learn'd Arguments that could be pen'd.

To shew their Loyalty, some they did Sign,
Others wav'd in their minds, but at last did decline
For to Go to the Barrack's their duty, to Do:
Over some Indians, who never were true.

There was Lawyers & Doctors, & Children in Swarms.
Who had more need of Nurses, than to carry Arms
The Q———s so peaceable as you will Find:
Who never before, to Arms were Inclin'd.

To kill the Paxtonians, they then did Advance,
With Guns on their Shoulders, but how did they Prance;
When a troop of Dutch Butchers, came to help them to fight,
Some down with their Guns ran away in a Fright.

Their Cannon they drew up to the Court House.
For fear that the Paxtons, the Meeting would force.
When the Orator mounted upon the Court Steps
And very Gentely the Mob he dismiss'd.

45

QUAKERS RESIST THE STAMP ACT AND THE TAX ON TEA

John Dickinson.

When Parliament for the first time imposed a tax on the American colonies "to defray the expenses of defending them" and adopted the Stamp Act of 1765, Quakers resisted as vigorously as anyone else. Most of the merchants of Philadelphia were Friends, and they did not hesitate to deny the right of the British government to levy such a tax. The merchants possessed the most powerful means of opposing the Stamp Act, a united resolution not to import British goods until the measure was repealed. Quaker merchants signed the non-importation agreement almost to a man.

At the Stamp Act Congress in Albany, N. Y., Quaker-born John Dickinson, of Philadelphia, took the lead and drafted the declaration of the Congress asserting "the undoubted right of Englishmen that no new tax be imposed upon them but with their consent."

Again in 1767, Quakers were in the forefront in resisting Parliament's tax on tea. John Dickinson was acclaimed a hero for publishing in newspapers his historic *Letters of a Farmer in Pennsylvania to the Inhabitants of the British Colonies.* Quaker merchants and attorneys served on the Committees of Correspondence formed for improving communication among the colonies. These Committees were the first effective steps toward unifying all American colonists. But Quakers at that time were not advocating war or revolution. They were claiming their rights as Englishmen.

TO THE
Delaware Pilots.

WE took the Pleasure, some Days since, of kindly admonishing you *to do your Duty*; if perchance you should meet with the *(Tea,)* SHIP POLLY, CAPTAIN AYRES; a THREE DECKER which is hourly expected.

We have now to add, that Matters ripen fast here; and that *much is expected from those Lads who meet with the Tea Ship.*----There is some Talk of A HANDSOME REWARD FOR THE PILOT WHO GIVES THE FIRST GOOD ACCOUNT OF HER.----How that may be, we cannot *for certain* determine: But ALL agree, that TAR and FEATHERS will be his Portion, who pilots her into this Harbour. And we will answer for ourselves, that, whoever is committed to us, as an Offender against the Rights of *America*, will experience the utmost Exertion of our Abilities; as

THE COMMITTEE FOR TARRING AND FEATHERING.

TWO SHIPS NAMED POLLY

The non-importation agreements applied to all cargoes from Britain, not just to tea. In 1769 when a vessel named *Charming Polly* arrived in Philadelphia with a cargo of malt, Quaker John Reynell, chairman of the merchants' committee, called a public meeting in the State House yard. All the brewers of the city were invited, most of them also being Quakers. The brewers agreed that they would not use any of the malt, and the crowd at the meeting resolved that anyone who would buy it "had not a just sense of liberty and is an enemy to his country." The *Charming Polly* sailed with the malt on board.

After the British East India Company was given an unpopular monopoly on the tea trade, it was resisted as vigorously as the tax. In every colonial port, merchants knew in advance when the tea shipments left England and which ships were bound for which ports. Philadelphians knew weeks ahead of time that the ship *Polly* was bringing 600 cases of tea consigned to two of the most prominent Quaker business houses, the firm of Thomas and Isaac Wharton, and that of Abel James and Henry Drinker. River pilots had been threatened with tar and feathers if they brought the ship to dockside.

Before the tea ships reached any of the colonial ports, Philadelphians organized another mass meeting at the State House on October 17, 1773, adopting a resolution which echoed the words of John Dickinson: "The duty imposed by Parliament upon tea landed in America is a tax on the Americans, levying contributions on them without their consent." Copies were sent to merchants in other ports, including Boston where a meeting in Faneuil Hall in October declared: "the sense of this town cannot be better expressed than in the words of certain judicious resolves lately entered into by our worthy brethren, the citizens of Philadelphia."

The Boston tea ship arrived first, but merchants there were prevented from following Philadelphia's example of the malt cargo. The Governor of Massachusetts refused to permit the ship to leave without unloading the tea. So citizen "volunteers" dumped the cargo into the harbor on December 16.

Ten days later word came that the *Polly* had reached the Delaware River. Before proceeding to Philadelphia the captain was persuaded to accompany a delegation of citizens to still another State House meeting on December 27. Eight thousand Philadelphians passed resolutions, the first of which was "the tea shall not be landed". Thomas Wharton took the captain home for dinner, lent him enough money to provision the ship for its return journey, and saw him off.

The Philadelphia tea party was somewhat more Quakerly than the one in Boston, but just as effective.

QUAKER—OR NOT A QUAKER?

John Dickinson is a classic example of problems often encountered by historians and genealogists: should he be identified as a Quaker?

He was brought up as a Quaker, worshipped at Friends meeting in his youth, and was taught Friends' principles by his Quaker parents. After leaving home at 18 to study law, he was separated from Quaker influence. But he married Polly Norris, daughter of Isaac Norris and granddaughter of James Logan, thus moving back into the very core of Philadelphia's Quaker community.

John and Polly Dickinson used plain language in their home. She was an active member of Meeting, and so were their daughters. Most people regarded John as a Friend, but there is no evidence he ever asked for or received a certificate of membership.

Dickinson's posture in public affairs was certainly the most Quakerly. He was author of the temperately-worded addresses sent by both the First and Second Continental Congresses to the King and Parliament. But when more radical delegates pressed for overthrow of British rule and Independence for America, his conscience would not let him go so far.

On July 1, 1776, Dickinson rose in Congress to take part in the debate over the resolution of Henry Lee, of Virginia. He delivered a restrained, well-reasoned speech arguing that Independence was not the right way to redress the colonists' wrongs.

Dickinson and fellow-Philadelphian Robert Morris stayed away from the State House on the crucial day of the balloting, enabling the rest of the Pennsylvania delegation to vote for Independence.

Dickinson retained the respect of his fellow citizens. He was chosen President of Pennsylvania, and President of Delaware after he retired to Wilmington. He was a member of the convention which drafted the United States Constitution. In his late years, Dickinson worshipped at Wilmington Friends Meeting House. He was buried, at his own request, in the graveyard there.

HISTORICAL SOCIETY OF PENNSYLVANIA

Dickinson's notes for his
speech opposing independence

CONGRESS AND THE QUAKERS

When the First Continental Congress met in Philadelphia in September, 1774, three members of Philadelphia Yearly Meeting were among the Pennsylvania delegates: Thomas Mifflin, one of the most outspoken of the Quaker merchants; Samuel Rhoads, long-time colleague of Franklin and builder of Pennsylvania Hospital; and Charles Humphrey, a miller from Haverford. These Friends had no difficulty joining other delegates in adopting The Association, an agreement for non-importation and non-consumption of British goods. Some more revolutionary-minded delegates wanted to go further, but it was decided to try one more conciliatory address to the King. John Dickinson drafted it. He had been made a delegate to replace Rhoads when Rhoads resigned to become Mayor of Philadelphia.

The First Congress adjourned in October, planning to meet again the next year "unless the redress of grievances which we have desired, be obtained before that time." Philadelphia Yearly Meeting was in session about then and felt some further effort at conciliation was needed. An epistle was addressed to all Friends in America reminding them that although past generations of Quakers had stoutly resisted laws they considered unjust, they had not participated in "plots or conspiracies." Friends, they said, had an obligation not to "excite disrespect or disaffection" for the King.

In January, 1775, another "Testimony" was prepared by Friends of Yearly Meeting, this one despatched to all citizens, not just to Quakers:

> We are, therefore, incited by a fincere concern for the peace and welfare of our country, publicly to declare againft every ufurpation of power and authority, in oppofition to the laws and government, and againft all combinations, infurrections, confpiracies, and illegal affemblies: and as we are reftrained from them by the confcientious difcharge of our duty to almighty God, " by whom kings reign, " and princes decree juftice," we hope through his affiftance and favour, to be enabled to maintain our teftimony againft any requifitions which may be made of us, inconfiftent with our religious principles, and the fidelity we owe to the king and his government, as by law eftablifhed ; earneftly defiring the reftoration of that harmony and concord which have heretofore united the people of thefe provinces, and been attended by the divine bleffing on their labours.
>
> *Signed in, and on behalf of the faid meeting,*
>
> JAMES PEMBERTON, *Clerk at this time.*

Still again in January, 1776, with Washington's army in the field and Congress directing war from the Pennsylvania State House, Yearly Meeting sent out "To the People in General" a summary of "The Ancient Testimony and Principles of the People Called Quakers" which concluded:

> May we therefore firmly unite in the abhorrence of all such writings, and measures as evidence a desire and design to break off the happy connection we have heretofore enjoyed, with the kingdom of Great Britain, and our just and necessary subordination to the king, and those who are lawfully placed in authority under him; that thus the repeated solemn declarations, made on this subject, in the addresses sent to the king, on the behalf of the people of America in general, may be confirmed, and remain to be our firm and sincere intentions to observe and fulfil.
>
> *Signed in and on behalf of a meeting of the Representatives of our Religious Society, in Pennsylvania and New-Jersey; held at Philadelphia, the 20th day of the first month, 1776.*
>
> JOHN PEMBERTON, Clerk.

Finally, the epistle least understood by Congress and widely denounced as "seditious" was issued by the Meeting in December, 1776. The Declaration of Independence had been adopted months before. At that very time, the British Army was advancing south from New York and the capture of Philadelphia was believed imminent.

> Thus we may with christian firmness and fortitude withstand and refuse to submit to the arbitrary injunctions and ordinances of men, who assume to themselves the power of compelling others, either in person or by other assistance, to join in carrying on war, and of prescribing modes of determining concerning our religious principles, by imposing tests not warranted by the precepts of Christ, or the laws of the happy constitution, under which we and others, long enjoyed tranquillity and peace.
>
> *Signed in and on behalf of the Meeting for Sufferings, held in Philadelphia, for Pennsylvania and New-Jersey, the 20th day of the Twelfth Month, 1776,*
>
> JOHN PEMBERTON, *Clerk.*

George Washington's crossing of the Delaware on Christmas night, 1776, saved Philadelphia on that occasion. But the sons of liberty remembered the several Yearly Meeting publications and used them the next year to denounce leading Quakers as traitors and enemies of the State.

NICHOLAS WALN AND BURHOLME

A section of northeast Philadelphia known as Burholme takes its name from the ancestral home of the Waln family in England.

The first American Waln, Nicholas, brought his family from there in 1682 with William Penn aboard the *Welcome*. He bought 1000 acres north of the city and built a house which was one of the early places of worship for the Friends group

which later became Abington Meeting. His great-grandson, also named Nicholas, was the attorney who guided many Friends during the years of the Revolution.

The second Nicholas, born in 1742, gained admittance to the bar before he was of age. He made himself fluent in the German language and built up the most lucrative law practice in the city by the time he was 30, principally by representing the many Rhinelanders who came to settle in Pennsylvania's rich farmland. But one day after attending a Youths' Meeting at Second and Market Streets, he abruptly abandoned his office to devote himself to the Society of Friends. James Logan's son, William, told about it in a letter to a friend:

> *"It may be new to thee, perhaps, to be informed that thy friend, my relation, Nicholas Waln, has, from being almost at the head of the law*

with us, in high esteem and great practice, from a very sudden and unexpected change, left the calling, and is likely to become a Public Friend."

Waln's knowledge and experience was invaluable to Friends in Philadelphia in dealing with their legal problems, but he never resumed active practice. His role was that of a quiet listener who was frequently able with a few words to suggest the solution to a problem. His style was to "dwell in love and keep low".

Nicholas Waln was one of the Overseers of the Friends public schools. Late in life he made lengthy religious visits as a Public Friend to England and to Ireland. He died in 1813 at age 71.

• • •

Nicholas Waln's niece, Hannah Waln, married Joseph Ryerss. It was their son, Joseph, who gave the name Burholme to the elaborate, Italian-style mansion which he built on a hillside in 1859. The name then spread to the neighborhood. In 1910, Robert W. Ryerss left the mansion and 50 acres of rolling meadow to the City of Philadelphia as a museum, library and public park.

Burholme Mansion—1859.
Named for the Waln ancestral home.

THE STORY OF ELIZABETH GRISCOM (BETSY ROSS)

One January night in 1776 ammunition exploded in a Philadelphia warehouse, mortally wounding John Ross, a young upholsterer who was on guard duty with the militia. He died shortly afterward in his nearby home while his bride of two years tried in vain to aid him.

She was Elizabeth Griscom Ross, a birthright Philadelphia Quaker known around the world now as Betsy Ross. Entirely aside from the flag story, she deserves to be better known in her own right as a woman of strength and courage during a long life of adversity.

Elizabeth Griscom was born in 1752. Her father, a carpenter, helped build the bell tower at the State

was "read out" of her Meeting "on account of her marriage to a person of another religious persuasion contrary to the advice of her parents and the good order used amongst us."

The newlyweds left Webster's shop and began an upholstery business of their own. They were barely started when John Ross was killed. Nevertheless, the 24-year-old widow determined to operate the shop herself. The story is that five months later, George Washington and a committee of Congress visited her to have her sew the first Stars and Stripes. This cannot be documented, but it is a fact that for more than 50 years, Elizabeth Ross continued to operate her own shop and to support herself and her family.

She married Joseph Ashburn, a ship captain whose vessel was captured by the British. For two

Marriage License of Elizabeth Griscom and John Ross.

House. Her mother was Rebecca James, of the prominent Quaker merchant family. Elizabeth attended Quaker schools and developed real skill in needlework. She went to work in the upholstery shop of William Webster and there met John Ross.

The young couple wanted to marry, but he was the son of an assistant rector at Christ Church. The Griscoms forbade the match. Elders from the Northern District of Philadelphia Meeting waited upon Elizabeth and threatened disownment if she should marry out of Meeting. The only result was that the two waited until both were 21, then eloped to Gloucester, N.J. by ferryboat to be married by James Bowman, an accommodating Justice of the Peace who frequently performed that service for young Philadelphians in the same situation.

The bride thereafter attended Christ Church where her pew is now marked for sightseers. She

years she had no word whatever, then learned that he had died in prison in England. After the war, she married John Claypoole, a soldier in the Continental Army who had been wounded in the Battle of Germantown. His health broke down in 1800, when she was only 48, leaving her to nurse him for a period of fifteen years while also managing the business. She continued until age 75, retired and died at 84.

Betsy and John Claypoole joined the Free Quaker Meeting when it was organized during the last years of the Revolution. She was buried in the Free Quaker graveyard. Not long ago, her body was transferred to a grave in the park adjoining the small house at 239 Arch Street which tradition says is where she lived and worked. Next to Independence Hall and the Liberty Bell, it is the most popular tourist spot in Philadelphia.

THE BATTLE AT BIRMINGHAM MEETING

Birmingham Meeting House, built 1763.

In a second campaign to capture Philadelphia, General Howe sailed from New York to the head of Elk River, Maryland, by way of Chesapeake Bay and then marched overland into Pennsylvania. George Washington established a line of defense on high ground overlooking the Brandywine, hoping to stop him there. But the American forces were defeated and Philadelphia occupied a week later.

The all-day battle on September 11, 1777 is called in history books the Battle of the Brandywine. The fighting took place in the fields and orchards of Quaker farmers and across the burying ground of Birmingham Friends Meeting. Residents of that Quaker neighborhood called it the Battle at Birmingham Meeting.

Washington placed the center of his defense line at Chadd's Ford on the main Nottingham Road (now Baltimore Pike). His army had marched long and hard to reach there, and some of his men were ill. He requisitioned Birmingham Meeting House to be used for a hospital. A 21-year-old member of the Meeting, Joseph Townsend, told what happened there on First Day (Sunday) September 7:

"Friends assembled as usual from an expectation that the meeting might be held in the house even if it should be taken possession of afterward; but from the situation of it, their request could not be granted. They therefore got permission to take some of the benches out of the house and placed them under the trees

which stood in front thereof, on which they seated themselves in the quiet as far as was practicable under the existing circumstances, inasmuch as the officers and workmen were moving about, and engaged in making preparation to receive the sick . . ."

• • •

As his headquarters for the forthcoming battle, Washington chose the roomy house of Benjamin Ring, an overseer of Concord Meeting at Concordville, north of Chadds Ford. Ring operated a mill nearby. A neighboring house belonging to Gideon and Sarah Gilpin was assigned to be headquarters for the Marquis de Lafayette.

Lafayette had only just arrived to join Washington's staff. He had been commissioned a Major General while still in France. He celebrated his 20th birthday in the week before the Brandywine battle.

• • •

Howe's army bivouaced the night of September 10, 1777 near Kennett Square, Pa. Next morning, Howe sent General Knyphausen with a force of 8000 German mercenaries directly up Nottingham Road as if to force a crossing there. Meanwhile, with an even larger body of troops under General Cornwallis, Howe circled to the north, marching all morning to cross the Brandywine above Chadds Ford, then turning south on Washington's side of the creek.

Old Kennett Meeting House—Built 1710—On Nottingham Road, now Baltimore Pike. CHESTER COUNTY HISTORICAL SOCIETY

Thursday, September 11 was the date for the monthly meeting at old Kennett Meeting House. As Knyphausen's soldiers marched by on the Nottingham Road, some of the first shots of the battle were exchanged with American scouts on the lawn of the meeting house. Friends did all they could to ignore the troops and the sounds of battle.

Present at the Kennett Meeting that morning was Jacob Peirce, the Quaker farmer-botanist whose arboretum was to become the nucleus of today's Longwood Gardens. Mindful of the advices of Yearly Meeting, he reported simply: "While there was much noise and confusion without, all was quiet and peaceful within."

Hannah Peirce, Jacob's sister-in-law, an invalid confined to her home, wrote in her journal nothing more than: "This day was a very trying time. The English army was marching through the neighborhood, and as it was the usual time for Kennett Monthly Meeting, it was difficult for Friends to get there."

• • •

Members of Birmingham Meeting assembled for mid-week worship that morning while the British army was making its way toward them. Unable to use their meeting house, they gathered in the wheelwright shop.

"While we were sitting therein, some disturbance was discovered near the house and about the door, which occasioned some indi-

viduals to go out to know the cause . . . and the uneasiness not subsiding, suspicions arose that something serious was taking place, and the meeting accordingly closed."

General Washington received confused intelligence reports about the British encircling movement. He swung the troops on his right around to face the redcoats advancing southward. The defense line was established at Birmingham Meeting House, with Americans using the walls of the burying ground as a breastwork. Washington and Lafayette rushed there and saw some of the fiercest fighting of the day.

When firing began at the meeting house, Knyphausen's soldiers at Chadds Ford forced a crossing of the Brandywine so that the two British forces threatened to crush the Americans between them. Washington ordered a retreat and was able to withdraw his troops toward Chester when Howe ordered his men to halt as evening approached.

General Howe established headquarters in nearby Dillworthtown. Birmingham Meeting House was used temporarily as a hospital before Howe resumed his advance into Philadelphia.

A stone marker in the burying ground of Birmingham Meeting indicates the common grave for the slain of both armies:

In memory of those who fell In the Battle of the Brandywine.

CONGRESS ORDERS QUAKER LEADERS ARRESTED

However well some members of the Continental Congress understood the peaceable neutrality of Quakers, a majority of delegates did not. On receipt of news that General Howe was in Maryland and headed toward Philadelphia, Congress called upon the States to take steps to prevent "disaffected" citizens "from pursuing measures injurious to the general weal." Everyone knew this meant Quakers.

JOURNALS OF CONGRESS, 1777.

TUESDAY, *August* 26, 1777.

...ea, That 10,000 ... .s . a..a..ced to the delegates of Mary... for the use of that state, which is to be accountable.

Whereas, the states of Pennsylvania and Delaware are threatened with an immediate invasion from a powerful army, who have already landed at the head of Chesapeake-Bay; and whereas, the principles of policy and self preservation require that all persons who may reasonably be suspected of aiding or abetting the cause of the enemy, may be prevented from pursuing measures injurious to the general weal:

Resolved, That the executive authorities of the states of Pennsylvania and Delaware, be requested to cause all persons within their respective states notoriously disaffected, forthwith to be apprehended, disarmed, and secured, till such time as the respective states think they may be released without injury to the common cause.

Resolved, That it be recommended to the supreme executive council of the state of Pennsylvania, to cause a diligent search to be made in the houses of all the inhabitants of the city of Philadelphia, who have not manifested their attachment to the American cause, for fire-arms, swords, and bayonets; that the owners of the arms so found be paid for them at an appraised value, and that they be delivered to such of the militia of the state of Pennsylvania who are at present unarmed, and have been called into the field.

Ordered, That the board of war furnish the state of Maryland with as many fire-arms as can be spared for arming their militia now called into service. The board

---

Distrust on the part of Congress turned to anger and recrimination two days later. John Hancock, President of Congress, received from American General John Sullivan a packet of papers said to have been seized from spies several days before on Staten Island. Included were messages purporting to show that the British had received intelligence about the size and location of Washington's military units sent by "Spanktown Yearly Meeting" in New Jersey.

No such Friends Meeting existed and the supposedly treacherous papers were entirely spurious. But Congress did not know that, and immediately suspected the worst. Hancock appointed a committee of three to investigate Sullivan's material. The chairman was John Adams, a delegate notoriously impatient with Quakers for their reluctance to fight for Independence.

Adams' committee concluded its investigation and submitted its report that very day, reviewing not only the "Spanktown" papers but also the various "Testimonies" which Philadelphia Yearly Meeting had been distributing for the past two years, much to the annoyance of ardent patriots. There is no evidence of any Quaker witnesses being called, but the committee's report named eleven leading members of Philadelphia Meeting and asserted "these persons maintain a correspondence and connection highly prejudicial to the public safety."

Congress approved the committee's report on the spot and immediately called upon the several states to "apprehend and secure" Quakers and others similarly evidencing "a disposition inimical to the cause of America."

THURSDAY, *August* 28, 1777.

...e advan... ...., commissary-general of mi...ary stores, 50,000 dollars, for the use of his department, for which he is to be accountable.

The committee to whom the letter from general Sullivan, with the papers enclosed, was referred, report,

"That the several testimonies which have been published since the commencement of the present contest betwixt Great Britain and America, and the uniform tenor of the conduct, and conversation of a number of persons of considerable wealth, who profess themselves to belong to the society of people commonly called Quakers, render it certain and notorious, that those persons are, with much rancor and bitterness, disaffected to the American cause : that, as these persons will have it in their power, so there is no doubt it will be their inclination, to communicate intelligence to the enemy, and, in various other ways, to injure the councils and arms of America :

That when the enemy, in the month of December, 1776, were bending their progress towards the city of Philadelphia, a certain seditious publication, addressed "To our friends and brethren in religious profession in these and the adjacent provinces," signed "John Pemberton, in and on behalf of the meeting of sufferings held at Philadelphia for Pennsylvania and New-Jersey, the 26th of the 12th month, 1776," was published, and, as your committee is credibly informed, circulated amongst many members of the society called Quakers, throughout the different states :

That, as the seditious paper aforesaid originated in the city of Philadelphia, and as the persons whose names are under mentioned, have uniformly manifested a disposition highly inimical to the cause of America, therefore,

Resolved, That it be earnestly recommended to the supreme executive council of the state of Pennsylvania, forthwith to apprehend and secure the persons of Joshua Fisher, Abel James, James Pemberton, Henry Drinker, Israel Pemberton, John Pemberton, John James, Samuel Pleasants, Thomas Wharton, sen. Thomas Fisher, son of Joshua, and Samuel Fisher, son of Joshua, together with all such papers in their possession as may be of a political nature.

And, whereas, there is strong reason to apprehend that these persons maintain a correspondence and connexion highly prejudicial to the public safety, not only in this state but in the several states of America,

Resolved, That it be recommended to the executive powers of the respective states, forthwith to apprehend and secure all persons, as well among the people called Quakers as others, who have, in their general conduct and conversation, evidenced a disposition inimical to the cause of America; and that the persons so seized, be confined in such places, and treated in such manner, as shall be consistent with their respective characters and security of their persons:

That the records and papers of the meetings of sufferings in the respective states be forthwith secured and carefully examined, and that such parts of them as may be of a political nature, be forthwith transmitted to Congress:"

The said report being read, and the several paragraphs considered and debated, and the question put severally thereon, the same was agreed to.

Ordered, That the board of war remove, under guard, to a place of security out of the state of Pennsylvania, the hon. John Penn, esq. and ...
... ...

THE VIRGINIA EXILES

Faced with the approach of Howe's army, Pennsylvania was no more forbearing with the Quakers than Congress—even though the President and the Secretary of the State's Executive Council both came from old Quaker families. They were out of union with the Meeting and out of sympathy with those who professed neutrality. They sent out deputies to round up all those on the list of "disaffected" received from Congress and other leading Friends as well.

The Council demanded that all those accused accept a "parole" and sign a pledge not to give intelligence to the enemy. Those who agreed to do so were left at liberty, but not all agreed. Some of the strongest minded insisted that as men of integrity and good character they had a right to know what charges were brought against them and to be given hearings at which they could defend themselves. But Council had no time for the fine points of justice. The dissenters were ordered taken into custody:

> *"Council would not without necessity commit many of the persons to the common jail or even the State prison. Congress recommended it and we wish to treat men of reputation with so much tenderness as the security of their persons and papers will permit."*

The Masons' Lodge—1777.

Council's "tenderness" sent those arrested to confinement in the new Masonic Lodge near Second and Walnut Streets. For about a week some of the Meeting's best-known members were held in gentle imprisonment. Families could visit; servants could attend to their needs; some were allowed overnight visits home. These niceties, however, did not overcome the outrage. From the moment of their arrest, the prisoners began bombarding the authorities and the public with remonstrances and protests against their treatment.

Council and Congress decreed that twenty of the recalcitrants, of whom 18 were Friends, should be banished, without any hearings, to prevent communication with the British Army. On September 11, 1777, with the sound of guns at Brandywine clearly heard in the city, the exiles were sent off in a guarded wagon train for Winchester, Virginia.

At first, the prisoners were closely guarded, but when it became obvious the Quakers would not attempt escape, they enjoyed considerable freedom. Some boarded with Quaker families in the neighborhood. They were able to worship at Hopewell and Center meeting houses near Winchester, both of which at that time were part of Philadelphia Yearly Meeting.

The many public protests and remonstrances drew no answer from the authorities, but eventually the innocence of the Quakers became obvious. They were not men who would pass military secrets to the British. After spending eight months in Virginia, the Quaker exiles were brought back to Pennsylvania and released. At that time, the King's army was still in possession of Philadelphia, but the Quakers were allowed to return to their homes—proof enough that charges against them were unfounded.

No official apology or restitution was ever forthcoming. A letter written to Congress by Thomas Wharton, Jr., President of the Council, was the closest to public recognition that wrong had been done:

> *"The affairs of the Commonwealth of Pennsylvania are so circumstanced as to admit the return of the prisoners sent from that State into Virginia without danger to the Commonwealth or to the common cause of America.*

> *"The dangerous example which their longer continuance in banishment may afford on some future occasions has already given uneasiness to some friends of the independence of these states."*

Hopewell Meeting House near Winchester, Virginia.

The Friends exiled in Virginia in 1777-78 included both "weighty" members of Philadelphia Yearly Meeting and some who seemed picked out almost at random as object lessons to the Quaker community:

The Pembertons: James, Clerk of Yearly Meeting; John, Clerk of the Meeting for Sufferings; Israel, their older brother, sometimes called "The Quaker Pope"; and Samuel Pleasants, husband of Israel's daughter.

The Fishers: Thomas and Samuel, merchants, and their lawyer brother, Miers; also, Thomas Gilpin, husband of their sister, Lydia.

Leading merchants: Henry Drinker, Clerk of Northern District of Monthly Meeting; Edward Pennington; Thomas Wharton, Sr. (Wharton was an older cousin of the President of the Council which ordered him banished.)

Five younger merchants: Elijah Brown, Charles Eddy, Charles Jervis, Owen Jones, Jr., William Smith.

John Hunt, a London Friend recently settled in Philadelphia and close friend of the Pembertons.

Thomas Affleck, the cabinetmaker, intimate of the Fisher family and favorite supplier of well-to-do Quaker families.

• • •

John Hunt and Thomas Gilpin both died during the period of exile and were buried at Hopewell Friends Meeting House.

To the PRESIDENT *and* COUNCIL *of* PENNSYLVANIA.

The REMONSTRANCE of the Subſcribers, Freemen, and Inhabitants of the City of *Philadelphia*, now confined in the Free-Maſon's Lodge.

SHEWETH,

THAT the Subſcribers have been by virtue of a Warrant ſigned in Council by George Bryan, Vice Preſident, arreſted in our Houſes, and on our lawful occaſions, and cond̲u̲c̲ed to this Place, where we have ̶ ̶ ̶ ̶ ̶ ̶ to charge them Confinement ̶ ̶ ̶ ̶ becomes of too great Magni̲ ̲ ̲ to be conſidered as the Cauſe of a Few.— It is the Cauſe of every Inhabitant, and may, if permitted to paſs into a Precedent, eſtabliſh a Syſtem of Arbitrary Power unknown but in the Inquiſition, or the deſpotic Courts of the Eaſt.—

give Evidence againſt himſelf; nor can any M̲ be juſtly deprived of his Libert̲ Laws of the I̲ ̲ ̲ ̲ P̲ ̲ ̲ ̲ ̲ ̲ emberton, *Thomas Wharton, Thomas Coombe, Edward Pennington, Henry Drinker, Phineas Bond, Thomas Gilpin, John Pemberton, Thomas Pike, Owen Jones,* junr. *Thomas Affleck, Charles Jervis, William Smith,* (broker,) *William Drewet Smith, Thomas Fiſher, Miers Fiſher, Charles Eddy, Iſrael Pemberton, John Hunt, Samuel Pleaſants.*

Maſon's Lodge, Philadelphia,
September 5th, 1777.

BRITISH REDCOATS IN PHILADELPHIA

General Howe's army which marched into Philadelphia in September, 1777, continued to hold the city until June. After the Battle of Germantown in October and the seige of Fort Mifflin in November, the British enjoyed long months of city living while Washington's soldiers were in winter camp at Valley Forge.

British officers were quartered in some of the finest homes in the city. The large house of Henry and Elizabeth Drinker on Front Street near the Bank Meeting House became the quarters of British Major John Crammond.

Elizabeth Drinker's Journal

October 24, 1777—*An officer called today to know if Gen'l Grant could have quarters with us; I told him as my husband was from me and a number of young children 'round me, I should be glad to be excus'd. He replied: as I desired it, it should be so.*

December 18—*Major John Crammond call'd this afternoon to look for quarters for some officer of distinction . . . I desir'd to be excused and after some more talk we parted. He behav'd with much politeness, which has not been the case at many other places.*

December 19—*Major Crammond came . . . I told him I expected that we who were at present 'lone women would be excus'd. He said he fear'd not, for tho' I might put him off (as it was for himself he applied to me) yet as a great number of ye foreign troops were to be quartered in this neighborhood, he believed they might be troublesome . . .*

Owen Jones's family has been very ill used indeed by an officer who wanted to quarter himself, with many others, on them. He drew his sword, us'd very abusive language and had ye front door split in pieces.

Mary Eddy has some with her who, they say, will not suffer to make use of her own front door, but obliges her and her family to go up and down the alley.

December 20—*Crammond call'd a third time with ye same story over again. I put him off as before . . . Mary Eddy call'd this afternoon in much affliction. She wanted Sister of myself to go with her . . . to make a complaint of one who has quarter'd himself on her and a woman he calls his wife, but Mary thinks otherwise. He has insulted her and behav'd very abusive.*

December 29—*Crammond here this morning. We have at last agreed on his coming to take up his abode with us. I hope it will be no great inconvenience, tho I have many fears.*

December 30—*One servant is to be with him here. Two others he has boarded at our neighbor Wells in ye alley.*

January 1, 1778—*J. C. has three horses, three cows, two sheep and two turkeys with several fowls in our stable. He has three servants, two white men and a Negro boy called Damon. Ye servants are here all day but away at night. He has three Germans who take their turns to wait upon him as messengers or orderlies as they are called, so that we have enough of such company.*

January 5—*J. C. had eleven or twelve officers to dine with him today.*

January 19—*This morning our officer moved his lodgings from ye blue chamber to ye little front parlor so that he has two front parlors, a chamber up two pairs of stairs for his baggage, and ye stable wholly to himself besides ye use of ye kitchen. His camp bed is put up.*

January 29—*Our major stayed out last night till between twelve and one. At a concert at headquarters. I fear he will do the same thing tonight as he is gone to an assembly.*

February 11—*I am out of all patience with our major. He stays out so late almost every night.*

February 17—*Our major had eight to ten to dine with him. They broke up in good time, but he is gone off with them and when he'll return, I know not. I gave him some hints two or three days ago and he has behaved better since.*

J. C. has tea with us today along with Samuel Emlen, Anthony Benezet, Robert Waln and others.

March 14—*Our major dined with us today for the first time.*

March 19—*Our major had a concert this evening, eleven of them in company. It was carried off with as much quietness and good order as the nature of the thing admitted of.*

March 20—*Our major took it into his head to dine today in the Summer-house with another officer. He had two or three to visit him while they sat there; so that when ye house is kept open, I suppose we shall have them passing and repassing, which has not been the case hitherto. They behav'd well and appeared pleased, but I don't feel so.*

(During April, Elizabeth Drinker was off on the journey to Lancaster)

May 8—*Sammy Sansom and J. Crammond spent the evening with us.*

May 13—*J. Crammond had a concert here this afternoon, seven or eight officers were with him, Dr. Knowles, one of them, came into our parlor and had some talk with my Henry. There is some movement in the army which we do not understand; ye heavy cannon are ordered on board ye ships, and some other things look mysterious.*

May 16—*Some of ye officers have orders to pack up their baggage.*

May 22—*Ye officers have orders to put their baggage on board ye vessels; our major packed up his matters today for that purpose.*

May 23—*Ye army, 'tis thought, is going in reality to leave us—to evacuate the city.*

May 24—*Ye officers' baggage going on board ye vessels all day; ye people talk confidently now of their leaving us.*

May 25—*Our major sent his things away this morning. He is at a loss, or appears to be, as are so many others, what to think of ye present appearance of things.*

May 30—*'tis reported that ye British army are giving the remainder of their stores of wood and hay to ye poor, which seems to prove they intend ere long to leave us.*

June 6—*Anthony Benezet, David Bacon, Dr. Redman and J. Crammond drank tea with us.*

June 8—*Orders given this day for two regiments of Germans to embark—our major goes with them . . . Ye major is very busy sending his things on board.*

J. Crammond supped with us; he is now gone to bed, to be called at one o'clock, to go off with his company . . . I intend to sit up till they are gone.

June 9—*Ye major left us at a little past one this morning. He was very dull at taking leave. Sister and self stayed at ye door, until ye two regiments (which quartered up town) had passed. J. C. bid us adieu as they went by, and we saw no more of him.*

• • •

October 28, 1781—*Heard from New York of the death of J. Crammond, a young officer who lived six months with us while ye British troops were in this city and behaved so in our family as to gain our esteem. He died after eight days illness—have not heard ye time exactly.*

These models of the Drinker house are on exhibit in Friends Meeting House, Fourth and Arch Streets, Philadelphia.

Elizabeth Drinker's journal for the day of
the visit to Washington at Valley Forge.

DINNER WITH GEORGE WASHINGTON

Four valiant Quaker women undertook a long and
difficult journey from Philadelphia to Lancaster on
their own in 1778, hoping to appear in person
before the Pennsylvania Council to plead for
release of the exiles in Virginia. Traveling in the
Pemberton family coach, drawn by two fine horses
and attended by a pair of well-mannered liverymen,
the delegation quite overwhelmed sentries guarding the American camp at Valley Forge.

Although they had no pass, the appearance and
demeanor of the women obtained passage from one
officer to another until they reached the winter
headquarters of General Washington himself:

> "We arrived about 1/2 past one, requested an
> audience with the General and sat with his
> wife (a sociable, pretty kind of woman) until he
> came in. A number of officers there who were
> very compliant, Tench Tilghman among ye
> rest. It was not long before G. W. came and
> discours'd with us freely, but not so long as we
> could have wish'd, as dinner was serv'd in, to
> which he had invited us.

> "There were 15 of ye officers besides ye General
> and his wife, Gen. Greene and Gen. Lee. We
> had an elegant dinner which was soon over,
> when we went out with ye Gen'ls wife up to her
> chamber and saw no more of him.

> "He told us he could do nothing in our business
> further than granting a pass to Lancaster,
> which he did."

Stopping at the homes of Quakers along the way
for noon-time dinners and overnight accommoda-
tion, the four ladies spent three more full days on
the road. The highways were muddy, the weather
rainy. At times, the two youngest Friends walked to
lighten the heavy coach and climbed fences to
avoid the mud. In Lancaster, they interviewed some
members of Council, but were denied any official
hearing. They learned that decision had already
been reached to bring the prisoners back to Pennsylvania and remained in Lancaster to meet them.

Those making a journey so extraordinary for
their day were Phoebe Pemberton, wife of Israel;
Molly Pleasants, wife of Samuel and daughter of
the Pembertons; Sarah Jones, mother of Owen, Jr.,
and Elizabeth Drinker, wife of Henry. The story of
their trip is told in Elizabeth Drinker's journal.

THE MASSACRE AT HANCOCK'S BRIDGE

The Hancock family of Salem County, N. J. originated with William Hancock, who came to Fenwick Colony in 1677 and owned a thousand acres on Alloway's Creek. The main road from Salem to Greenwich ran through the property and John Hancock in 1708 built a bridge which was given his name. Close by the crossing, John's son William and his wife Sarah built "a commodious brick dwelling" which is still standing, its west wall displaying their initials and the date 1734. The wall is ornamented also with the zig-zag pattern in blue glazed brick characteristic of Salem County.

By 1778, the house at Hancock's Bridge was owned by the builder's son, William Hancock, a Quaker and a Judge. He helped build Alloway's Creek Friends meeting house. Because of the events which transpired there on the night of March 21, 1778, the house is now preserved by the State of New Jersey as an historic site.

· · ·

Anthony Wayne made a successful raid into South Jersey in March, 1778, for food and supplies for the troops at Valley Forge. British units stationed in Salem failed to capture him and thereafter made retaliatory sallies into the surrounding countryside. They were twice defeated by Jersey militia at Quinton's bridge over Alloway's Creek, then planned a surprise night attack upon militia guarding Hancock's bridge further upstream.

As guides, the British commanding officer used "Jersey Volunteers", American Tories who had fled to Salem and joined the enemy. They knew the territory well. The assault was made early in the morning of March 21 after the British had traveled from Salem by boat under cover of darkness.

Asleep upstairs in the 1734 house were Judge Hancock and three other elderly members of Allo-

way's Creek Friends Meeting. Downstairs was headquarters for about 20 militiamen assigned to guard the bridge. A contemporary journalist's account tells the story:

> "Our guard of about twenty men were surprised by those the enemy call Jersey Volunteers; They, from their acquaintance with the country had found means to cross the creek and come upon the guard from some unsuspected quarter; and being undoubtedly led by some person well acquainted with the disposition of sentries, opened the guard-house door and came in, many of the guard being asleep, without giving the least alarm, nay, so far from it, that it is said some of them shook hands in a friendly manner with some of the guard with whom they were intimately acquainted . . .

> "They immediately began bayoneting of them, without our people making the least show of resistance, not only reeking their fury on the guard but also on several of the peaceable inhabitants who were slumbering in their beds . . . Old Mr. Hancock, besides his being of the Society called Quakers, was a cripple in both his arms, was stabbed in his bed and is since dead of his wounds."

Not a shot was fired. All three of the Quaker civilians died along with Judge Hancock. None of the surprised militiamen escaped alive.

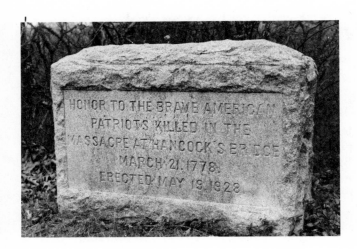

THE STORY OF LYDIA BARRINGTON (Lydia Darragh)

On entering Philadelphia, General Howe first moved into the home of John Cadwalader, a rich merchant, on the west side of Second Street below Spruce. Later he occupied the Market Street mansion where Governor Penn had lived and which later served as President Washington's White House. When Howe moved out, however, officers of his staff remained in the Cadwalader house.

Across the street lived the Darraghs, a family of Irish Quakers. In Ireland William Darragh had been a tutor in the home of John Barrington. He and Lydia Barrington were married in Dublin Friends Meeting in 1753, coming to America and being well settled in 1777 in Loxley Hall, a dwelling named for its builder, the colorful Captain Benjamin Loxley.

The tradition is that early in December a British officer from across the street asked the Darraghs to let him use their house for a conference, that Lydia Darragh listened in on the meeting and learned that an attack was being planned on Washington's army then stationed in Whitemarsh, north of Philadelphia.

Loxley Hall.
Residence of Lydia Barrington Darragh in 1777.

Under pretense of going out of town to purchase flour, it is said, Lydia walked several miles until she found an American soldier and thus conveyed a message of warning to headquarters. There is substantial evidence to support this much of the story. But those who tell the tale usually claim that Lydia Darragh's bold exploit saved Washington's army from destruction, and that is not true.

During the night of December 4, 1777, a large force of British did march out of Philadelphia and approach the Americans at Whitemarsh. They found Washington well prepared for battle, maneuvered in the area for two days, then returned to the city without attempting any major engagement. Historians cite documentary proof that advance warnings had reached the American headquarters from several sources.

Does that discredit Lydia Darragh?

It is a fact that one of the officers of Howe's army was Captain William Barrington, of the Royal Seventh Regiment. He was Lydia's cousin and he was in Philadelphia. Might he not have asked the use of her house?

Moreover, American General Elias Boudinot has written:

> *"In the autumn of 1777 the army lay at Whitemarsh. I was Commissary General and managed the intelligence of the army. I dined at a small post at the Rising Sun, about three miles from the city.*

> *"After dinner a little, poor-looking, insignificant old woman came in and solicited leave to go into the country to buy some flour. While we were asking some questions, she walked up to me and put into my hands a dirty old needle-book with various small pockets in it . . ."*

General Boudinot wrote that inside the last of the pockets he found a rolled-up piece of paper with a message that the British were coming out of Philadelphia with 5000 troops and 13 cannon.

> *"On comparing this with other information, I found it true and immediately rode post to headquarters."*

STRANGE GOINGS-ON AT A QUAKER MANSION

"The Mischianza" was an extravagant, ostentatious and absurd pageant staged by British officers in honor of General Howe when he was leaving Philadelphia in May, 1778.

After a full-dress parade with military bands through the streets and a showy procession by boat on the Delaware, fourteen mounted British officers, accompanied by squires and heralds, staged a mock tournament with lance and sword to proclaim the beauty and wit of their favorites among the young ladies of Philadelphia. Looking on were the daughters of some of Philadelphia's best families in costumes and head-dress reminiscent of King Arthur's court.

The tournament was followed by all-night dancing, a sumptuous midnight supper, fireworks and cannon salutes. Of itself, the Mischianza was unimportant, but it is mentioned in every history of Philadelphia because the British major who staged it wrote a lengthy account of every detail for the *Gentlemen's Magazine* of August, 1778. He was John Andre, the brilliant and artistic young officer later hanged for his part in the treason of Benedict Arnold.

Invited to the extravaganza and listed in the printed guest list which Major Andre thoughtfully prepared, were three daughters of Chief Justice Edward Shippen. Family tradition is, however, that just before the event a committee of Friends from Philadelphia Meeting called upon the Judge and persuaded him to keep the sisters at home.

Still, there was a Quaker connection with the Mischianza. As the most appropriate place for their jousting and night-long revelry, the British officers chose "Walnut Grove", the estate of Friend Joseph Wharton, a solid member of Meeting who had died a year or so before. His house was unoccupied. Were it standing today, it would be near the intersection of Fifth and Wharton Streets.

Walnut Grove.
House of Joseph Wharton.

63

TWO QUAKERS HANGED IN PHILADELPHIA

Within a week after the British army evacuated Philadelphia in June, 1778, both Congress and the Executive Council of Pennsylvania moved back into the city. The days and weeks which followed were for many Quakers the worst of the war. Council seemed determined to find and to punish some of those who had remained in the city during the occupation—Quakers as well as others. Repeated proclamations accused hundreds of "knowingly and willfully" aiding the enemy and ordered them to stand trial for treason.

A special court was set up in Philadelphia and trials were run off one after another in rapid succession. Most of those accused were acquitted or pardoned. Not many were executed, but among those who did go to the gallows were two Quakers, Abraham Carlisle and John Roberts.

Philadelphia, November 7.

Last Wednesday was executed on the commons of this city, according to their sentence, John Roberts and Abraham Carlisle. The unhappy prisoners behaved with the greatest resolution.

Last Sunday a son of mr. Andrew Burkhard's, of this city, was baptised by the name of Joseph Reed, in honor of the worthy patriot of that name.

ABRAHAM CARLISLE

A carpenter of modest circumstances, Abraham Carlisle, age 58, belonged to Northern District Meeting and was a neighbor of Henry Drinker, the Meeting Clerk. A newspaper report said: "Whilst the British had possession of the city, he was one of the inhabitants appointed to attend at the gates, to allow only particular persons to go out of the lines, and see that no goods were carried out that there was not a permit for from the superintendent's office."

Friends said Carlisle's principal function was to issue passes to poor people desiring to go into the country to buy flour. But the prosecutor said he had allowed British spies to leave the city to reconnoiter in the American-held countryside. Carlisle was found guilty of high treason on September 26.

JOHN ROBERTS

The situation differed greatly in the case of John Roberts, age 55. He belonged to Merion Meeting and was a wealthy owner of mills for grinding grain, sawing lumber and making paper located on what was then called Roberts Mill Creek. (now Mill Creek).

Roberts was accused of leaving his home, meeting General Howe's army after the Battle of Brandywine, and urging that a force of British soldiers be sent to rescue the Friends who were being sent in exile to Winchester. He remained with the British throughout the occupation of Philadelphia, but did not flee with the British to New York, as many Tories did. He surrendered himself for trial and argued in defense that while in Philadelphia he had used his influence with General Howe to relieve some of the misery of American prisoners there.

Roberts, too, was convicted. Chief Justice Thomas McKean in sentencing him said:

> "It is in vain to plead that you fled to the enemy for protection against some of your neighbors who threatened your life because they thought you a Tory; for you might have applied for and obtained protection from the civil magistrate, or from the army of your own country . . .

> "It is in vain to plead that you intended to re-lieve some friends who were ordered under guard to Virginia, for Government was then doing a necessary and usual act for its preser-vation . . .

> "Your offering to put yourself at the head of a troop of horse of the enemy, and to effect this rescue at the risk of your life, was a strange piece of conduct in one who pretended that he was conscientiously scrupulous of bearing arms in any case. Alas, happy had it been for you, had you fallen under the like indulgent restraint and been also sent to Virginia.

> "It is true, and I mention it with pleasure, that your interest with the commander-in-chief of the British army was frequently employed in acts of humanity, charity and benevolence. This must afford you some comfort, and your friends some consolation . . . but can by no means compensate for treason."

• • •

Elizabeth Drinker knew both Carlisle and Roberts. The former, as a neighbor, had often called to comfort her while her husband was at Winchester. She had stopped overnight with Roberts' wife and their daughters on the trip to and from Lancaster that Spring. The Drinker journal contains this record:

October 24, 1778—John Roberts and Abm Carlisle's death warrant was signed today and read to them.

October 28—Jane Roberts, wife of John Roberts; Owen Jones and wife, and James Thornton were here this morning. H. D. and self went with them to visit our neighbor, Ann Carlisle. James had something to say to ye afflicted women by way of testimony which I thought encouraging. Ye time for execution of their husbands is fix't ye 4th next month.

November 3—I was informed that preparations were making this evening for ye execution of our poor Friends tomorrow morning, nothwithstanding the many petitions that have been sent in, and ye personal appearances of ye distressed wives and children before ye Council. I am still of ye mind that they will not be permitted to carry this matter to ye last extremity.

November 4—They have actually put to death—hang'd on ye Commons—John Roberts and Am. Carlisle this morning or about noon. An awful, solemn day it has been. I went this evening with my H. D. to neigh'r Carlisle's. Ye body is brought home and laid out . . . Ye poor afflicted widows are wonderfully upheld and supported under their very great trial. They have many sympathizing Friends.

November 5—H. D. left home this morning for Radnor Meeting, intending tomorrow for Merion where I expect he will be at ye funeral of John Roberts. Our back parlor was filled this afternoon with company who came to ye burial of our neig'r Carlisle. Myself and four children went. It was a remarkable large funeral and a solemn time. George Dilwyn and S. Emlen spake at ye grave, and ye former prayed feverently."

Philadelphia Prison—1778.
Carlisle and Roberts were held here in "The Stone Prison" while awaiting execution. At Third and Market Streets, it was only a block from The Great Meeting House.

THE FREE QUAKERS

While the great body of Philadelphia Yearly Meeting sought to live by "the ancient principles" and to avoid the struggle for Independence, some members were led by their consciences to join in it, just as others, fewer in number, assisted the British.

Thomas Mifflin, a leading Quaker merchant in Philadelphia, became a General and commissary chief in Washington's army. Samuel Morris served as Captain of the mounted troop which served as Washington's bodyguard, the colorful unit which is still active as the First City Troop. A few less prominent Friends served as soldiers in the ranks and in such capacities as blacksmiths and wagon drivers.

Among the "Fighting Quakers" were found such other well-known names as Biddle, Dickinson, Marshall, Matlack, Wetherill and Wharton. These were not leaders of Philadelphia Meeting, and the Meeting had no sympathy for their stand. One by one in a steady flow, those who went to war and those who accepted offices under the revolutionary government, were "read out" of their monthly meetings. Often they continued to join in Friends worship and their families to remain members of Meeting.

One of the approved ministers of Philadelphia Meeting was Samuel Wetherill, a chemist and druggist. The meeting disowned him in 1779 because he had "deviated from our ancient testimony and peaceable principles by manifesting himself a party in the public commotions prevailing." The next year he gathered around him a group of seven other Friends in similar situation and formed a new meeting, the "Free Quakers."

From the Monthly Meeting of FRIENDS,

Called by Some

The FREE QUAKERS,

Held by Adjournment at Philadelphia, on the 9th Day of the 7th Month, 1781.

To those of our Brethren who have disowned us.

BRETHREN,

AMONG the very great number of persons whom you have disowned for matters religious and civil, a number have felt a necessity of uniting together for the discharge of those religious duties, which we undoubtedly owe to God and to one another. We have accordingly met and having seriously considered our situation, agreed to establish and endeavour to support, on the ancient and sure foundation, meetings for public worship, and meetings for conducting our religious affairs. And we rejoice in a firm hope, that as we humble ourselves before God, his presence will be found in them, and his blessing descend and rest upon them.
As ... h ... by your proceedir ... against ... s separated yourselves from ... s, and declared

Denied the use of existing meeting houses, the Free Quakers built one of their own in 1783 at Fifth and Arch Streets in Philadelphia. Their meeting never grew large, and when the war was over and the United States of America firmly established, the reason for separation ended. Samuel Wetherill and Elizabeth Claypoole (Betsy Ross) were the last members.

The State of Pennsylvania restored the Free Quaker Meeting House and made it part of today's Independence Mall. It is now the oldest meeting house in downtown Philadelphia. The Society of Free Quakers still exists, too, as a corporation but not as a religious organization. Reeves Wetherill, the present Clerk is a descendant of the first. The Society meets annually to distribute endowment income for charitable purposes.

Free Quaker Meeting House, Fifth and Arch Streets, Philadelphia.

"THE QUAKER REVOLUTION"

The Quaker scholars, Isaac Sharpless and Rufus Jones, wrote that the war for Independence was "a revolution not less in Quaker development than in American history."

The role of Philadelphia Yearly Meeting and its members changed entirely from what it had been for a century before. Friends no longer managed the government of Philadelphia and Pennsylvania. They sought deliberately to leave public affairs to others, concentrating upon reformation of their own Society. The goal was a return "to primitive zeal, plainness and circumspect walking amongst the professors of Truth."

"The Revolutionary War left Philadelphia Yearly Meeting more moral internally, more devoted to moral reforms, more conservative of ancient tradition, custom and doctrine, more separate from the world, more introspective in spirit, than it found it . . .

"Had the active, public-spirited Friends, who went off with the revolutionary movement, remained to mould their generation, a type more outward, more progressive, more intellectual would have resulted . . .

"Had the Society drifted along as it was drifting prior to the conflict, a moral stringency, since characteristic of Quakerism, could hardly have been maintained. As a result of the combined narrowing and uniting processes, Friends are what they are."

PRESIDENT WASHINGTON WRITES TO PHILADELPHIA MEETING

Quakers quietly accepted the new government established under the Constitution of 1787. Philadelphia Yearly Meeting sent a message of good will to Washington upon his election as first chief executive. The President replied with equal graciousness, although he could not overlook "their declining to share with others the burden of the common defense".

"Gentlemen:

"I receive with pleasure your affectionate address, and thank you for the friendly sentiments and good wishes which you express for the success of my administration, and for my personal happiness.

"We have reason to rejoice in the prospect that the present national government, which by the favor of Divine Providence, was formed by the common counsels, and peaceably established with the common consent of the people, will prove a blessing to every denomination of them.—To render it such, my best endeavors shall not be wasting.

"Government being, among other purposes, instituted to protect the persons and the consciences of men from oppression, it certainly is the duty of rulers, not only to abstain from it themselves, but according to their stations, to prevent it in others.

"The liberty enjoyed by the people of these states, of worshipping Almighty God agreeable to their consciences, is not only among the choicest of their blessings, but also of their rights.—While men perform their social duties faithfully, they do all that society or the state can with propriety demand or expect; and remain responsible only to their Maker for the religion or the mode of faith which they may prefer or profess.

"Your principles and conduct are well known to me, and it is doing the people called Quakers no more than justice to say that (except for their declining to share with others the burden of common defense) there is no denomination among us who are more exemplary and useful citizens.

"I assure you very explicitly that in my opinion the conscientious scruples of all men should be treated with great delicacy and tenderness, and it is my wish and desire that the laws may always be as extensively accommodated to them, as a due regard to the protection and essential interests of the nation may justify and permit."

G. WASHINGTON

THE STORY OF DOROTHEA PAYNE (DOLLEY MADISON)

After her Quaker parents moved from Virginia to Philadelphia, Dorothea Payne, 22 years old, married John Todd, Jr. under the care of Pine Street Meeting. He was the son of a Quaker schoolmaster and a rising young lawyer. They bought a house which is still standing at Fourth and Walnut Streets.

For three years all went well. Then came the yellow fever epidemic of 1793. John Todd and both his parents died. So did one of the two sons which had been born to the young couple. Dorothea survived, a widow with a young child. Within a year a new chapter in her life began. Philadelphia was then the capital of the new nation. The President and Martha Washington lived only two blocks away from the Todd home. Congress and the Supreme Court were sitting at the State House. The social life of the city was astir with distinguished personages from all the states. One day, Dorothea Todd sent an excited message to her friend, Eliza Lee: "Thee must come to me. Aaron Burr says the great little Madison has asked to be brought to see me."

Aaron Burr was United States Senator from New York, and James Madison, "Father of the Constitution" was a Congressman from Virginia. He was 17 years older than Dorothea, but before the year was out they were married. They moved to Washington when the new "Federal City" was ready, Madison serving as Secretary of State under President Thomas Jefferson.

Since Jefferson was a widower, Dorothea Payne Todd Madison was called upon to be White House hostess. She won a reputation for her charm and grace, serving throughout Jefferson's two terms and then as the nation's First Lady for eight more years when James Madison succeeded Jefferson as President.

Dorothea was almost always called by her nickname, but she had a habit of spelling it two different ways—sometimes "Dolley" and sometimes "Dolly". When her little brick house in Philadelphia was made part of Independence National Historical Park, historians of the National Park Service studied all the available documents and concluded that the preferred spelling is "Dolley."

Dorothea Payne.

The First Lady,
Mrs. James Madison.

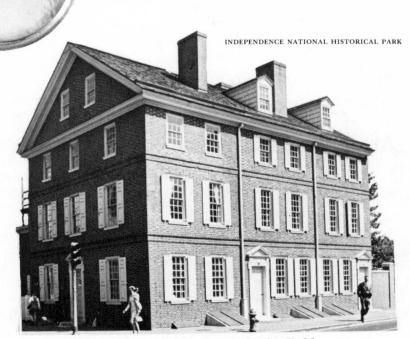

On the corner, the home of Dorothea and John Todd.

QUAKER CRAFTSMANSHIP

Philadelphia Yearly Meeting included among its membership two centuries ago not only merchants, physicians and lawyers, but also skilled artisans of many crafts. Today their work is handed down with pride in the families for whom it was produced and eagerly sought after by museums throughout the country.

CROSSWICKS CHAIRS

PHILADELPHIA MUSEUM OF ART

Chairs with barley-twist turnings like this one were turned out as early as 1690 in Crosswicks, a Quaker settlement near Burlington in West Jersey. This one is made of American black walnut. It was purchased by the Philadelphia Museum of Art after being found "in a forgotten corner of the attic of one of the oldest houses in the neighborhood."

THE HENRY FRANCIS DUPONT
WINTERTHUR MUSEUM

WILLIAM SAVERY

Many of Philadelphia's leading Friends purchased furniture from the shop of William Savery located just around the corner from the Great Meeting House at Second and Market Streets. Savery turned out everything from simple rush-bottom maple chairs to elegant chests and high chests of carved mahogany. The Savery name is also perpetuated through the career of a son of the cabinetmaker, also named William, who was a widely-travelled Quaker minister and preacher. Other descendants included the owners of the Savery farm in Chester County which has been transformed into Crosslands, the Quaker retirement community.

DANIEL TROTTER AND EPHRAIM HAINES

STEPHEN GIRARD FURNITURE COLLECTION
GIRARD COLLEGE, PHILADELPHIA

Philadelphia's wealthest citizen, Stephen Girard, was a customer of the Quaker furniture-makers, Daniel Trotter and Ephraim Haines. Trotter made this desk for Girard's home. Haines, a Friend from Burlington, served as apprentice in Trotter's shop, married Elizabeth Trotter, and inherited the business in 1800. Among his work for Girard was an unusual suite of parlor furniture made of ebony. The cathedra which is still used at historic Christ Church in Philadelphia was made by Haines for America's first Episcopal Bishop William White.

THOMAS AFFLECK

Unlike Savery, who served his apprenticeship in Philadelphia, Thomas Affleck arrived in the city in 1763 already an experienced journeyman. He was introduced to the Quaker community by the influential Fisher family and soon was making furniture for some of the finest homes in the city. This high-chest is a prize example of his work. The graceful sofa was made for Governor John Penn and was later purchased by Chief Justice Benjamin Chew. Thomas Affleck was one of the Friends banished to Winchester in 1777. He is said to have earned his board by making furniture there.

FURNITURE FOR CONGRESS

For the ten years that Philadelphia was the nation's capital while the city of Washington was under construction, the city turned over to the Federal Government the State House and the two adjoining buildings, the court house and the city hall. At least three Quaker craftsmen were employed to help get the buildings properly furnished for their distinguished new occupants. John Letchworth and Joseph Henzey, Sr. were employed to make new Windsor chairs for many of the offices. Thomas Affleck made desks and upholstered chairs for Congress Hall. Some of Affleck's original chairs are still to be seen in the Senate Chamber.

PHILADELPHIA MUSEUM OF ART
GIVEN BY CAROL WOOD STRETCH

PHILADELPHIA MUSEUM OF ART
GERMANTOWN TRIBUTE FUND

QUAKER CLOCKMAKERS

These examples of the skill of Quaker artisans of the 18th century are all now museum pieces. The severely plain one at the left came from the shop of Peter Stretch about 1710. There had been considerable change in style by the time Edward James made the case in the center half a century later. The third clock was made by David Evans during the period following the Revolution. He was the best known of the three.

WINDSOR CHAIRS

Windsor chairs were in fashion around the time of the Revolution, and Philadelphia was the center of their manufacture. Quaker artisans shipped thousands of them to ports up and down the Atlantic coast. Philadelphia Monthly Meeting might even be said to have been a partner of some of them.

For years, beginning with Joseph Henzey, Sr. and Joseph Henzey, Jr., successive firms of chairmakers rented a building on the property of the Bank Meeting House. Aware that chair-making would produce plenty of scrap wood, the Meeting wrote into the lease a provision that tenants had to supply it without charge and keep fires burning in the meeting house on days of worship. Later, it was provided that tenants not only had to keep the fires but furnish other custodial services as well, not just for Bank Meeting House but for several other places of worship.

The plainness of the simple Windsor chairs appealed particularly to Quaker craftsmen. John Letchworth, one of the earliest manufacturers, was a traveling Friends minister for most of his life.

PHILADELPHIA MUSEUM OF ART
GIVEN BY LYDIA THOMPSON MORRIS

72

THE GOVERNOR PENN CHAIRS

Thomas Affleck received a commission from Governor John Penn to make a set of twelve fine upholstered arm chairs. Although the set was broken and widely scattered at a sale of Penn's furniture in 1788, eleven of the twelve chairs have been traced and are are now on exhibit as works of art: two in the Philadelphia Museum; two in the Diplomatic Reception Rooms of the State Department in Washington; two at the Winterthur Museum in Delaware; one at Colonial Williamsburg; one at the Metropolitan Museum in New York; and one in the Bayou Bend Collection, Houston, Texas.

As for the two others among the eleven chairs known still to be in existence, they ended up in the most appropriate spot of all. These two were purchased by Quaker businessman Samuel W. Fisher when Thomas Penn sold the set in preparation for returning to England. Fisher retained them until 1817 when Quakers who were able to do so were asked to provide furnishings for the about-to-be-opened Friends Hospital. He donated his Penn chairs, which graced the Managers' Parlor of the institution for more than a century and a half.

In 1977, Friends Hospital offered to sell the two chairs to a suitable purchaser. Since at that time the National Park Service had just completed the restoration of the second floor of the Pennsylvania State House (Independence Hall) including the grand Council Chamber where Penn and his advisers used to meet, this seemed by far the most appropriate new home for the chairs. Funds were raised by a citizen's group, Friends of Independence National Historical Park, and Thomas Affleck's chairs presented. They are now arranged before the fireplace in the Governor's Council Chamber.

PHILADELPHIA FRIENDS AND THE INDIANS

After Friends no longer controlled the government of Pennsylvania, it was their custom to send representatives to sit in as observers whenever Indian treaties were being made to make sure that no unfair advantage was taken. Thus, William Savery and four other Philadelphians were present at Lake Canandaigua in New York in 1794 when George Washington's Secretary of State, Timothy Pickering, undertook to negotiate a treaty of friendship with the Six Nations of Iroquois Indians. At that time it was vitally important to the United States to make sure of the friendship of Indians living between New York and the British in Canada.

another Friend, started a school for Indian girls in 1825. The two teachers were married. When Elkinton returned to Philadelphia in 1831, he began a "soap and candle manufactory" which under the operation of his descendants became the Philadelphia Quartz Company.)

The Indian Committee of Philadelphia Meeting helped the Senecas in 1838 in a celebrated court case that upset a fraudulent "sale" which might have deprived them of their reservation in violation of the 1794 treaty. Again in the 1960s, Philadelphia Quakers rallied to aid the Senecas when the U.S. Army Engineers proposed a dam on the Allegheny

The Long House of the Seneca Indians in New York State bears architectural resemblance to the meeting houses of their long-time allies, the Philadelphia Quakers.

One of the provisions of the Pickering Treaty promised that the Seneca Indians would be forever undisturbed on their land along the Allegheny River.

That negotiation was the start of a special relationship which still exists between Friends of Philadelphia Yearly Meeting and the Senecas of New York State. The Meeting at that time created the Indian Committee which has continued active service ever since. At the request of the Seneca chieftain Cornplanter, several Indian youths, including Cornplanter's son, were brought to Philadelphia to learn to read and write, and some Philadelphia Quakers were sent to the Seneca reservation to teach English and useful arts. Philadelphia's Indian Committee purchased 700 acres at Tunesassa, adjacent to the reservation, and maintained a school for Indians for more than a century.

(Joseph Elkinton, a Philadelphia Quaker, opened a boys' school there in 1822, and Mary Nutt,

Philadelphia Friends join Seneca Indians protesting construction of the Kinzua
Dam which flooded much of the land guaranteed to them by a treaty of 1794.
Philadelphia Quakers aided the Senecas in negotiating the original treaty.

River which would flood much of the Seneca reservation. It was argued that the dam took Seneca land without their consent and therefore violated their rights under the Pickering Treaty.

The effort to block construction of the dam was unsuccessful, but through a nation-wide campaign, Friends were able to help the Senecas receive greater compensation for their land and financial assistance in relocating their homes.

George Heron, president of the Seneca Nation,
reports to members of the Indian Committee at
the 1961 session of Philadelphia Yearly Meeting.

GRANT'S "PEACE POLICY"

President Ulysses S. Grant, convinced that warfare would never solve the nation's Indian problems, turned to the Society of Friends for leadership in establishing a new national "Peace Policy." Quakers from Philadelphia and other Yearly Meetings formed the Associated Executive Committee of Friends on Indian Affairs and, at the President's request, picked the Quaker leaders who became the first administrators of new Indian agencies. Orthodox Friends took responsibility for the Central Superintendency and its agencies in the Oklahoma and Kansas territories, while the Hicksites managed the President's policy in the Northern Superintendency, the Nebraska area. Later, other religious groups were asked to take part in the "Peace Program."

After the Grant Administration, Quaker heads of Indian agencies were gradually replaced by political appointees. The Associated Committee thereafter established its own programs for Indian assistance independent of the government agencies. To this day, four Quaker Indian missions or centers in Oklahoma are financed and operated under the Committee's care. Philadelphia Yearly Meeting is represented on the Associated Committee and contributes its share to support the four centers.

Philadelphia Friends Meeting House—Orthodox—1828

ORTHODOX AND HICKSITE

Philadelphia Yearly Meeting was split in two by "The Great Separation" of 1827. For more than a century, Friends were divided into two groups—Orthodox and Hicksite—with two monthly meetings existing in most Quaker communities and two Yearly Meetings in Philadelphia.

Unlike schisms in other religious societies, the division among Friends was not a basic one of doctrine or liturgy, but primarily a revolt within the business organization of the Society, a secession of country Friends from the establishment run by the group of "weighty Friends" in Philadelphia who were accustomed to exercise the authority of the Meeting.

The disagreement centered around two strong and unyielding personalties—Elias Hicks, a traveling Friends minister from Long Island who had become a regular visitor in the more rural monthly meetings of Philadelphia and Baltimore Yearly Meetings, and Jonathan Evans, leader of the more conservative Friends in Philadelphia.

At the Yearly Meeting of 1827, the two sides were unable to agree even on selection of a Clerk. Afterwards, John Comly, a Byberry schoolteacher and leader of the Hicksites, announced that his group had withdrawn. Several Meetings in the city and suburbs followed, as did most Friends in the more rural monthly meetings. New monthly meetings were established. Usually whichever side was in the majority continued to hold the existing meeting house, while those of the other view eventually built a separate place of worship. Schools, too, were divided, for neither group would entrust education of the young to the other.

In Philadelphia, Orthodox Friends retained the Arch Street Meeting House. Hicksites raced to put up their own meeting house three blocks away on Cherry Street between Fourth and Fifth Streets, completing it in just 66 working days. In the meanwhile, they met in historic Carpenters' Hall.

After two or three generations, the bitterness of the separation passed and it became largely a matter of custom and precedent. By the turn of the century, first steps were being taken in the direction of unity, particularly among young Friends. But it took another half century before the complex situation could be untangled and complete unity accomplished by a formal juncture of the two Yearly Meetings into one in March, 1955.

Philadelphia Friends Meeting House—Hicksite—1828.

ARCH STREET AND RACE STREET

Hicksite Friends outgrew their first meeting house on Cherry Street and in 1856 erected the double meeting house west of Fifteenth Street with space for the Monthly Meeting on the Cherry Street side and a larger room for Yearly Meeting facing Race Street. For the next hundred years, the two separate divisions of Friends were usually identified by the addresses of their meeting houses—the Orthodox being "Arch Street Friends" and the Hicksites, "Race Street Friends."

ORTHODOX

HICKSITE

After 128 years of separation, Philadelphia's two branches of Friends achieved unity again in March, 1955. This photograph records the memorable occasion when the two former Meetings assembled for their first combined session in the meeting house at Fourth and Arch Streets. Speaking from the facing benches is Charles J. Darlington, of Woodstown, N.J. and at his right, James F. Walker, of Westtown School. They were Presiding Clerks for the first year of the merger.

Consolidation of the two separate Meetings had been inevitable for some time. Five years before, a joint "Committee of Organic Union" had been formed to work out agreement on the innumerable details. Friends from both sides were joined in a Philadelphia General Meeting to work toward unity. United Meetings already existed in many communities.

On Friday, March 25, 1955, the Yearly Meeting of the Religious Society of Friends of Philadelphia and Vicinity (Orthodox) met separately for the last time in the Arch Street meeting house. Simultaneously, the Philadelphia Yearly Meeting of Friends (Hicksite) held its final session at Fifteenth and Race Streets. Each Meeting formally approved the final steps of consolidation. On Monday, March 28, Friends met together for the first time under the name Philadelphia Yearly Meeting of the Religious Society of Friends.

FRIENDS JOURNAL

One evidence of the new unity among Philadelphia Quakers was the birth of a new publication, *Friends* *Journal.* It replaced *The Friend* (Arch Street) founded in 1828 and *Friends Intelligencer* (Race Street) founded in 1844.

QUAKER SILVERSMITHS

Three generations in one Quaker family— Francis Richardson, Joseph Richardson and Joseph Richardson, Jr.—made silver pieces for wealthy families in Philadelphia for 130 years.

Francis Richardson (1681 to 1729) established the family business in 1701, one of his first products being a pair of silver shoe buckles for Letitia Penn. The second Richardson, Joseph (1711-1784) became the most famous. He was followed by Joseph, Jr. (1752-1831) who continued the shop all his life and in addition served by appointment of President Washington as assayer of the United States Mint in Philadelphia.

Specimens of the fine work of all three Richardsons are pictured in every authoritative work on American silver. One of the outstanding pieces at the Philadelphia Museum of Art is this elegant teapot made by Joseph Richardson, Sr. about 1760. Its first owner was also a Quaker, Elizabeth Sandwith Skyrin, a niece of Elizabeth Drinker, the journal-keeper.

Mrs. Thomas J. Curtin, who presented this teapot to the Museum, is a sixth generation descendant of its maker and has herself earned a reputation as a talented silversmith.

PHILADELPHIA MUSEUM OF ART
GIFT OF MRS. THOMAS J. CURTIN

DAVID BECKWITH TAYLOR, JR.
LELAND, MISSISSIPPI
PHILADELPHIA MUSEUM OF ART PHOTOGRAPH

• • •

At its adjournment in October, 1774, the First Continental Congress voted fifty English pounds for purchase of a gift of silver for its secretary, Charles Thompson. The commission to make an appropriate item was given to Richard Humphreys, a 24-year-old Quaker who had just taken over the shop of the great Philip Syng, Jr. He produced this handsome tea urn which introduced the neoclassical style in America. It proved to be the major work of his long and successful career.

Richard Humphreys was an elder in the Pine Street Meeting. He was a founding director in 1784 of the Mutual Assurance Company for Insuring Houses from Loss by Fire (Green Tree) which is still in business. When he died in 1832 he left money to found a school for teachers, the Institute for Colored Youth, which has now become Cheyney State College.

The Charles Thompson urn is still in private hands, but numerous examples of Richard Humphreys silver are on exhibit at the Philadelphia Museum of Art and elsewhere.

QUAKER NEEDLEWORK

Fine quilts and samplers made by Quaker girls and women years ago are now prized as family heirlooms and museum pieces just as much as the work of Quaker cabinetmakers.

This large and colorful autograph quilt was completed in 1844 by members of the Female Society for Relief of the Distressed, a benevolent organization formed in 1793 by Ann Parrish and some of her young Quaker companions to aid families which had been victims of the yellow fever epidemic. In 1798, the Society opened a House of Industry, which provided work and wages for needy women for more than a century. The Society still exists, its programs now carried on through the Philadelphia Center for Older People.

Each member of the Female Society made and signed a square for this quilt which was presented to Ann Burns, matron of the House of Industry, upon her retirement after forty years service. It is now on exhibit in the meeting house at Fourth and Arch Streets.

South Jersey family quilting party

This delicate sampler of needlepoint lace was made by 12-year-old Jane Humphreys in 1771. She was the daughter of the Philadelphia ship-builder, Joshua Humphreys. Although a member of Friends Meeting, he is sometimes called the Father of the United States Navy because his ship designs were used in making the country's most successful warships.

This patchwork quilt in the traditional "sunburst" pattern was made in 1839 by Rebecca Scattergood Savery, then 69 years old, for the birth of her first granddaughter, Sarah Savery. It has 3903 diamond-shaped patches of cotton chintz.

Rebecca's son, Thomas, and his wife, Hannah Webb Savery, became the owners of "Ellerslie", the Chester County farm on which the Quaker-sponsored retirement community, Crosslands, is now situated.

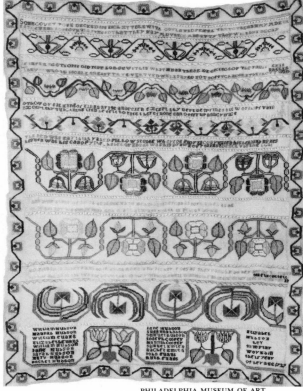

Several samplers similar to this one dated 1737 are still in existence, all made by teen-age daughters of prominent Quaker families apparently while students at a Friends school. This one was executed by Elizabeth Hudson, granddaughter of a Colonial Mayor of Philadelphia, during her fifteenth year.

QUAKER WEDDINGS

Among all the ancient Quaker ways of life, two which have come down to the present day almost unchanged are the silent meeting for worship of God and the Quaker marriage ceremony.

Although young Friends are no longer disowned for "marrying out of Meeting" or for "marriage by a hireling priest," those who do choose to be married under the care of a Friends Meeting are expected to follow the procedures handed down by old-time Friends.

Bride and groom notify the Meeting of their intentions and are interviewed by committees appointed to ascertain their "clearness" for marriage. Thereafter, the proposed marriage must "pass" two sessions of the Meeting for Business at least a month apart. After the date for the wedding is set, a special Meeting for Worship is appointed, within which the marriage takes place.

At the appointed Meeting, bride and groom take their places on the facing benches, with or without a wedding party. Perhaps an overseer or elder explains the nature of the Friends ceremony for the benefit of any not familiar with it. A period of silent worship follows. The couple rise, take each other by the hand and make their marriage promises to each other. A further time of silent worship passes, and perhaps some of those present speak or offer prayer.

Before the Meeting is broken by a handshake of overseers, the wedding certificate is brought to the newly-marrieds for their signatures, after which the lengthy certificate is read aloud testifying that the marriage has been accomplished "in accord with the good order used among Friends." Later, the certificate is signed by all in attendance.

A special form of wedding license must be obtained in some states for Quaker marriages, since there is no clergyman to sign the portion of the usual form returned for official records. That service is performed for Friends by overseers.

"In the presence of God and these our friends, I, _____ take thee, _____ to be my wife, promising with Divine assistance to be unto thee a loving and faithful husband so long as we both shall live."

Howard Pyle, Quaker-born artist, writer and teacher, produced "A Quaker Wedding" to illustrate an article in Harper's Magazine in December, 1885. It has since become a classic, the original hanging in the Friends Historical Library at Swarthmore College. Pyle lived in Wilmington. He was the originator of the Brandywine School of painting, his pupils including N. C. Wyeth, Violet Oakley and Maxfield Parrish. He died in 1911.

After the bride and groom sign it, the wedding certificate is read to the meeting.

QUAKER ROMANCE—1821-1837

GARRETT SCATTERGOOD HOAG

Edward and Abigail Sellers Garrett.

Darby Meeting House.

Edward Garrett, 21 years old, lived and worked on the family farm acquired by his great-great-grandfather from William Penn in 1684. One day in 1821, after he had finished his chores, Edward made this note in the daily journal which he and many young Quakers were taught to keep:

> *"This day as I drove to market I overtook Abigail Sellers on her way to school and gave her a ride in my apple cart.*
>
> *"Resolved: if it be the Lord's will, to make her my wife when she is old enough."*

Since Abigail was only twelve at the time, it was not a matter to be rushed. But sixteen years later, on November 19, 1837, Abigail Sellers and Edward Garrett were married in Darby Friends Meeting House. The place was most appropriate, since Abigail's Sellers ancestors had been the first couple married under the care of Darby Meeting 153 years before. The marriage continued until Edward's death in 1863. Abigail survived until 1881. Their descendants are numerous.

• • •

The Garrett homestead remained standing in modern Drexel Hill until demolished in 1969 for a school playground. It was located on Shadeland Avenue not very far from the busy highway which is named for the family, Garrett Road.

• • •

Abigail's family home, Sellers Hall, built before 1700, is still in existence, situated not very far away from the Sixty-Ninth Street transit terminal in Upper Darby.

Garrett homestead—Demolished 1969.

This former Quaker dwelling became the first chapel and rectory for the new Saint Alice Catholic parish when the Archdiocese of Philadelphia purchased some of the Sellers land during the real estate boom of the 1920s which transformed Upper Darby farm land into a well-populated suburb. Mass was said here regularly until a chapel could be built. After that, Sellers Hall served for a while as the rectory. Now it is still in use as the Saint Alice parish library.

EDWARD HICKS AND THE PEACEABLE KINGDOM

The painting shown here was sold in Philadelphia in April, 1980, for $210,000. It is but one of sixty or more variations of the same subject—*The Peaceable Kingdom*—executed by Edward Hicks, a Quaker preacher and member of Philadelphia Yearly Meeting.

Hicks is now celebrated as a genuine primitive painter, with museums the nation over bidding for copies of his work, but he was never regarded as an artist in his lifetime. He was an artisan, a painter of outdoor signboards for taverns and inns. He was in financial straits most of his life. When he died in 1849, the newspapers referred to him only as "an eminent minister of the Society of Friends."

ABBY ALDRICH ROCKEFELLER FOLK ART CENTER, WILLIAMSBURG, VIRGINIA

Edward Hicks was born in Bucks County, Pennsylvania, in 1780. His mother died when he was 16 months old. He was raised on the farm of well-to-do Quaker neighbors, David and Elizabeth Twining. At age 13 he was apprenticed to a coach and sign painter. Fifty years later, near the end of his life, he painted from memory this scene of his earliest years. He is the youngster standing at the side of Elizabeth Twining, who has a Bible in her lap. David Twining is the plain-garbed farmer in the foreground.

Life with the Twinings for more than ten years led Hicks to join Middletown Friends Meeting in 1803, the year of his marriage to Sarah Worstall. The Hicks family had been Episcopalian.

The leopard with the harmless kid laid down.
And not one savage beast was seen to frown.

The wolf did with the lambkin dwell in peace.
His grim carniv'rous nature there did cease;

The lion with the fatling, on did move,
A little child was leading them in love,

When the great PENN his famous treaty made
With indian chiefs beneath the ELM tree's shade.

By the time he was 30, Hicks felt it was his "duty" to preach. He moved to Newtown and in 1815 helped found Newtown Monthly Meeting.

As early as 1820, Hicks began producing his long succession of paintings based on the Old Testament verses from Isaiah:

> *"The wolf shall dwell with the lamb, and the leopard shall lie down with the kid; and the calf and the young lion and the fatling together; and a little child shall lead them."*

Along with his Biblical figures, Hicks placed a small rendition of what he considered a symbol of The Peaceable Kingdom—Penn's Treaty with the Indians. In this particular painting he added as well his own verses telling the story from Isaiah and paying tribute to Penn.

In the Quaker separation of 1827, Edward Hicks was a vigorous partisan of his first cousin, Elias Hicks.

Instead of the Penn Treaty scene, Hicks at this time substituted a pyramid of Quaker figures. Three at the summit are said to represent George Fox, William Penn and Robert Barclay, the leading Friends theologian. In the front row, holding a handcherchief, is Elias Hicks, and beside him, in the center, George Washington—no Friend, but a leader whom Hicks greatly admired. Carried by this distinguished group is a long banner or streamer which seems to link them to a heavenly company on a mountain behind them: "Behold I bring you glad tidings of great joy: peace on earth and good will to men."

THE STRANGE FRIEND OF LONDON GROVE MEETING

A man named Henry Cox moved into East Marlborough Township, Pennsylvania, with his wife and fourteen children in 1813. He rented one of Isaac Pennock's large tenant farms on Street Road a mile east of London Grove Friends Meeting. Thereafter he attended meeting for worship and regularly sat on the facing benches although he rarely spoke.

Cox did not exactly fit into that rural community. He was a man of Irish birth with courtly manners, cultured speech and a stiff military bearing. Obviously used to a different lifestyle from most Pennsylvania farmers, he was, nevertheless, a good farm manager who taught his neighbors some new and improved methods of crop cultivation.

After four years, Cox suddenly announced he was packing up his family and going to Ireland. The minutes of London Grove Meeting report: "Our Friend, Henry Cox laid before the Meeting a prospect he has of taking a voyage to Europe and requested something by way of certificate to show Friends where his lot may be cast that he is a member of our Society." The meeting provided this, addressed "To Friends in Dublin or Elsewhere". Shortly afterward Cox moved away, never to be seen or heard from again.

There were rumors that Cox had returned to his homeland to claim an estate he had inherited. Most members of Meeting concluded that he really had never been a Friend at all.

Years later, through books and documents he had given to the Library Company of Philadelphia, the Library learned that Cox was really a member of a titled family, a retired Army officer and great-grandson of a Chancellor and Chief Justice of Ireland. He had inherited a large but debt-ridden estate and had come to America to live incognito in simple style until the income from the property would amount to enough to free it from debt. Apparently the Society of Friends just suited his purpose.

We do not know whether Cox's neighbors at London Grove ever learned these facts. In 1868, however, a fictional story called "The Strange Friend" appeared in Atlantic Magazine. The author, Bayard Taylor who lived in the neighborhood, based his imaginary tale on what he had heard about Cox. He wrote that the Irishman used the name Henry Donnelly in the United States and that he turned out to be "Lord Dunleigh, of Dunleigh Castle in Ireland."

Some years after that, a member of London Grove Meeting bought the farm where Cox lived. He built from his own plans a large mansion quite unusual for that part of the country and named it "Dunleigh Castle". You can see it today as you drive along Street Road. The word "Dunleigh" is carved in a large stone directly over the front entrance.

The mansion named for a
fictional London Grove Friend.

London Grove Meeting House
and the great oak which was there before
Pennsylvania was founded.

SILHOUETTES

Many old-time Quakers who considered it vain and improper to have a portrait drawn or painted had no compunction whatever about posing for a silhouette. These were basically shadows, therefore "natural" and entirely seemly. As a rule, silhouettes are much more dependable likenesses than drawings or paintings made by friends from memory after the death of the subject. Some of these silhouettes portray real persons whose lifetimes spanned the years from the 1700s to the 1900s. Others are merely decorative art. Many are from Anna Cox Brinton's booklet *Quaker Profiles*.

THE SANSOM FAMILY

William Sansom, a member of Philadelphia Meeting, was an investor in real estate during the early 1800s. He and several partners bought a large tract of land between Walnut and Market Streets and between Seventh and Eighth. Some of it was then a pasture. Sansom cut through the street which now carries his name and there built eighty houses—the first row homes in Philadelphia.

This silhouette, made by the celebrated artist Edouart in 1843, portrays Sansom's widow, Hannah, her two daughters and a family servant bringing them a letter. Edouart usually carried with him printed indoor or outdoor backgrounds upon which he mounted his silhouettes, this making his work easier and also accounting for the inconsistency of the Quaker costumes and some of the parlor furnishings.

GEORGE VAUX.

86

M. HARLAN BYE

MARY SULLIVAN PATTERSON

Rosalie Bye.

ROSALIE BYE'S "QUAKERS"

Rosalie Paxson Bye was a talented Wilmington Quaker who not only painted pictures and cut silhouettes but also designed and made applique pictures of Quaker men and women in old-style costumes. These became much sought after in gift shops as presents for hostesses or for brides in Quaker weddings. Rosalie Bye continued to make them long after she moved into the Concord Friends Boarding Home in West Chester.

Rosalie Bye is well remem-bered by her relatives and a few friends still residing at the Home. She was a spirited lady who, although quite deaf, indignantly refused to wear a modern hearing aid. They describe her rocking contentedly in her favorite chair holding in one hand her after-dinner cigarette and in the other an old and battered tin ear trumpet. She died in 1949 at the age of 96. Two of her attractive "Quakers" are displayed in the building where she lived.

87

FRIENDS AND SLAVERY

GERMANTOWN FRIENDS' PROTEST AGAINST SLAVERY, 1688.

THIS IS TO Yᴱ MONTHLY MEETING HELD AT RICHARD WORRELL'S.

These are the reasons why we are against the traffick of men-body, as followeth. Is there any that would be done or handled at this manner? viz., to be sold or made a slave for all the time of his life? How fearful and faint-hearted are many on sea, when they see a strange vessel,—being afraid it should be a Turk, and they should be taken, and sold for slaves into Turkey. Now what is this better done, as Turks doe? Yea, rather is it worse for them, which say they are Christians; for we hear that ʸᵉ most part of such negers are brought hither against their will and consent, and that many of them are stolen. Now, ᵗʰᵒ they are black, we cannot conceive there is more liberty to have them slaves, as it is to have other white ones. There is a saying, that we shall doe to all men like as ᵗᵉ will be done ourselves; making n⁻ difference of ʷʰat generation, descent or colour they are. And ho s⁻...

The first public protest against slavery in America came from the tiny Friends Meeting in Germantown in 1688. The Clerk of the Meeting, Francis Daniel Pastorius, lawyer and schoolmaster, was the leader of the thirteen Germantown families who had emigrated in 1683. They were dismayed that slavery should exist in William Penn's province:

> "There is a saying that we shall do to all men like as we will be done ourselves; making no difference of what generation, descent or color they are. And those who steal or rob men, and those who buy or purchase them, are they not all alike? . . .

> "Here is liberty of conscience, which is right and reasonable; here ought to be likewise liberty of ye body, except of evil-doers, which is another case. But to bring men hither, or to rob and sell them against their will, we stand against . . ."

The Friends of Germantown were far ahead of their time. Neither George Fox nor William Penn had gone so far. The monthly meeting which received the protest concluded: "we find it so weighty that we think it not expedient for us to meddle with it here, but do rather commit it to ye consideration of ye Quarterly Meeting. . . ." The Quar-

terly gathering, in turn, recommended it to Yearly Meeting, "it being a thing of too great weight for this meeting to determine." Yearly Meeting in September, 1688, minuted:

> "A paper being here presented by some German Friends concerning the lawfulness and unlawfulness of buying and keeping negroes, it was adjudged not to be so proper for this Meeting to give a positive judgment in the case, it having so general a relation to many other parts, and therefore at present they forbear it."

Nevertheless, the seed had been planted. By 1696, the Yearly Meeting recorded: "It is the advice of this meeting that Friends be careful not to encourage the bringing in of any more negroes." In 1730 Yearly Meeting declared new slave purchases to be "disagreeable to the sense of this meeting," and by 1758 it decreed: "If any professing with us should be concerned in importing, selling or purchasing slaves, the respective monthly meetings to which they belong should manifest their disunity with such persons."

Friends were well ahead of the general population in acknowledging the evil of slavery. By the time of the Revolution, slave-holding was ended among Friends.

THE UNDERGROUND RAILROAD

Merely to do away with slave holding within their own ranks did not satisfy all Quakers. In 1780, Pennsylvania became the first State to abolish all slavery within its borders (through a gradual process). Thereafter some Quakers worked toward abolition throughout the United States, while others devoted themselves to helping runaway slaves make their way north on the Underground Railroad. Its traffic was heavy with passengers brought into southeastern Pennsylvania from Virginia, Maryland and Delaware.

Delaware was a slave state, but some Friends in Delaware regularly helped shelter runaways during daytime and transport them at night from one household to another on the journey northward. John Hunn, of Middletown, and Thomas Garrett, of Wilmington, were among the most active. A biographer estimates that Garrett provided refuge, guides and transportation for 2700 black fugitives during 25 years of activity as an underground "conductor."

Thomas Garrett.

THE TRACKLESS TRAIL

John Cox.   Hannah Cox.

THOMAS B. TAYLOR

The Cox homestead, a station on the Underground Railroad.

Most often, slaves sheltered by Thomas Garrett at his home at Third and Shipley Streets, Wilmington, were carried across the Pennsylvania line to the homes of Quaker farmers in the area of Kennett Square, chief among them Hannah and John Cox, whose home, "Longwood", was on the Nottingham Road not far from old Kennett Meeting House. From there, the route was usually through Philadelphia where the son of a slave family, William Still, was agent and later Secretary of the Pennsylvania Anti-Slavery Society.

Assisting runaway slaves to escape was, of course, illegal. Not all Friends approved the operation of the Underground Railroad. Nor did they agree when the more active anti-slavery Friends began bringing into Quaker meeting houses the most fiery abolitionist preachers from New England and elsewhere. Disownments of many Friends followed, and in 1854 a group who had been excluded from their own meetings formed a new Progressive Friends Meeting with a meeting house on part of the Coxes' Longwood farm. The meeting house is still standing near the entrance to Longwood Gardens, although it is no longer used for religious worship. Across the road is the old Longwood burial ground with graves of many Friends who were active in the years that the Underground Railroad flourished.

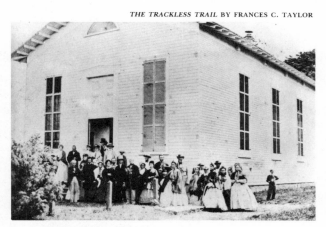

THE TRACKLESS TRAIL BY FRANCES C. TAYLOR

Longwood Meeting House—1895.

Lucretia Mott.

LUCRETIA MOTT

The leading woman abolitionist in the United States was a tiny, dainty, determined Quaker lady named Lucretia Mott. When she died in 1880, Philadelphia's *Evening Bulletin* said of her:

"She will be remembered through all time by Americans as one of the foremost of the brave little band of men and women who dared to do right when public opinion was wrong."

Seal of the
Female Anti-Slavery Society.

Born on Nantucket Island in 1793, Lucretia Coffin attended Friends School in New York State, began teaching there at age 15, married a fellow teacher, James Mott, at 18 and settled in Philadelphia. James Mott was a Quaker of principle, a textile merchant who at considerable personal sacrifice discontinued handling cotton because of its connection with Southern slavery. After the third child of their marriage died in infancy, Lucretia returned briefly to teaching at Friends Select School. She retained a lifelong interest in education and in later years took an active part in the organization of Swarthmore College.

Both James and Lucretia Mott were abolitionists. They attended formation of the American Anti-slavery Society in Philadelphia. Thereafter, Lucretia Mott organized and headed the Female Anti-Slavery Society. The two of them went to London in 1840 to attend the World Anti-Slavery Convention only to find that women were not permitted to sit as delegates. Elizabeth Cady Stanton, a recent bride, 25 years younger than Lucretia, also was barred from the convention. Eight years later the two women launched the women's rights movement at Seneca, New York. Lucretia Mott was later President of the American Equal Rights Association.

After the Civil War, Lucretia Mott became a leader in the peace movement and served as President of the Pennsylvania Peace Society.

For all her many interests, Lucretia Mott was a model wife and homemaker, mother of five children who lived to maturity, grandmother of twenty, a tidy housekeeper and a gracious hostess who regularly entertained as many as fifty in the Mott home before or after meetings in which the Motts were interested.

Executive Committee of the Pennsylvania Anti-Slavery Society. Lucretia and James Mott are at the right in the front row.

FRIENDS AND EDUCATION

The Society of Friends has always fostered education of young people—girls as well as boys, poor as well as affluent, non-Quakers as well as Quakers. William Penn hired the first schoolmaster for Philadelphia in 1683. Today, within Philadelphia Yearly Meeting territory there are 34 Friends schools—two boarding schools, ten high schools or preparatory schools, 13 elementary schools, and nine kindergartens or nursery schools.

Enrollment is not limited to Quaker children at any of the schools. Because of their academic excellence and widespread community respect for the principles on which they are founded, Friends schools all attract a high percentage of non-Quaker students.

Each year's campaign of the Friends Education Fund raises money for generous scholarships awarded through the Yearly Meeting's Committee on Education. In the school year 1979-80, financial aid was provided for 237 students in Friends schools, of whom 152 were children of Friends and 85 non-Friends. Schools of the upper grades participate in programs admitting disadvantaged youth in urban neighborhoods and foreign exchange students.

Friends Academy, 1763.

Germantown Friends School, 1866.

Early School bus.

Abington Friends School—Founded 1697.

First Day morning at George School.

91

PENN CHARTER SCHOOL

Philadelphia Monthly Meeting established schools long before the introduction of public education. At first the Meeting itself handled all details of running them. Later William Penn and his deputy issued charters for "The Overseers of the Public School Founded by Charter in the City and County of Philadelphia." For two centuries, these Overseers managed numerous schools under the care of Philadelphia Meeting.

When public-supported education reduced the number of Quaker schools, all were combined into one called The William Penn Charter School. In 1875 it opened in a residence adjoining the Meeting House on Twelfth Street near Market. After 50 years at that location, Penn Charter moved to its present location on School House Lane in Germantown.

WILMINGTON FRIENDS SCHOOL

When Wilmington Monthly Meeting moved to its second meeting house in 1748, it opened a school in the old one across the street. For almost two centuries the school remained there, its growing needs requiring frequent additions and renovations of the old 1738 meeting house. Finally, Wilmington Friends moved to its present location on a 50-acre campus in Alopocas, just outside the city.

FRIENDS' CENTRAL SCHOOL

Opened in 1845 near the meeting house at Fourth and Cherry Streets, Friends' Central moved to Fifteenth and Race Streets when the present Race Street Meeting House was erected in 1856. Since 1925 the school has occupied the old Wistar Morris estate on City Line, Overbrook. Philadelphia's Friends Center now occupies the Fifteenth Street site.

GERMANTOWN FRIENDS SCHOOL

Germantown Monthly Meeting opened this school in 1845. It is still located next to the meeting house on West Coulter Street, Germantown. The Meeting also created for its school a library which, with the help of generous Quaker donors, has now grown into the Friends Free Library of Germantown with its own ample building on Main Street next to the school. In keeping with a restriction imposed by one of its benefactors, the library contains no novels or other fiction except children's stories.

MOORESTOWN FRIENDS SCHOOL

This large school established by Friends in Moorestown, N.J., in 1785 is now preparing to celebrate its bicentennial. It serves not only Moorestown but several other communities in the Quaker territory of old "West Jersey" which was settled before Philadelphia. The Moorestown Meeting's School Committee includes representatives from other nearby monthly meetings, among them Haddonfield, Medford and Westfield. The present building was opened in 1929.

WESTTOWN SCHOOL, 1799

In 1799, primarily for the benefit of children from rural areas where Friends schools did not exist, Philadelphia Yearly Meeting opened "a central boarding school" modeled after the Ackworth School of English Friends. The necessary money was raised by subscription among members of Meeting, and the School Committee purchased a 600-acre farm in Westtown Township, Pa. Westtown School still occupies the same location and is still managed by a committee of Yearly Meeting. Part of the original farm land is still cultivated, producing a modest net income.

One of the principal roads leading to Westtown School is still called "Johnny's Way," the name given it years ago by students who trudged along it to reach the old-fashioned shoemaker's shop of John Fitzpatrick. "Johnny" was a genial, homespun philosopher who made friends with several generations of students while he mended their footwear. His portrait now hangs in Westtown's halls, and his low wooden shoemaker's bench is preserved in Westtown's Treasure Room.

THE GUMMERE SCHOOL

Quaker teachers in the old days often opened their own private schools, independent of those under Meeting care. One of the most celebrated was that opened in 1814 by John Gummere at Burlington, N. J. His reputation brought students even from foreign nations. He was the progenitor of a long line of Quaker educators still making academic history.

John Gummere served as first head of Haverford College when it opened in 1833, closing his own school to do so. His son, Samuel Gummere, a faculty member at Haverford, served as President there for eleven years. One grandson, Henry V. Gummere, was acting President of Haverford on two occasions during his long tenure as Director of the Strawbridge Observatory there while another, grandson, Francis B. Gummere, was a distinguished Haverford professor of English for 31 years.

Great-great grandson John Flagg Gummere attended Haverford as an undergraduate, but taught at Penn Charter School and became Headmaster there, serving from 1941 to 1968. Now Headmaster Emeritus, he has been a leader in many Friends educational organizations as well as Board Chairman of the National Association of Independent Schools.

QUAKER COLLECTION, HAVERFORD COLLEGE LIBRARY

GEORGE SCHOOL

John M. George

Since Orthodox Yearly Meeting had charge of Westtown School, Hicksite Friends wanted to establish a second boarding school under their care. There were long delays, including the years of the Civil War, but the project became possible when John M. George died in 1887 leaving his entire estate to the Meeting for that purpose. George was the elderly last member of a Quaker family which had owned a large farm in "Blockley Township" since the days of William Penn. Much of the present Overbrook section of Philadelphia is now built on the George farm which constituted the largest asset of John M. George's $700,000 estate.

More than 100 different locations for the George School were considered by the School Committee before a farm of 227 acres near Newtown, Pa. was chosen. Friends made it their rule to place boarding institutions in the country where it was easier to insure "a guarded education" for the students. George School opened in 1893 and graduated a class of ten in 1895.

George School still occupies its original location. The historic Twelfth Street Meeting house from Philadelphia now serves for meetings for worship and for special lectures and conferences.

TOUGHKENAMON BOARDING SCHOOL

Typical of many smaller Quaker boarding schools was one established in 1868 by Hannah M. Cope near her home in the Chester County community of Toughkenamon. One roomy old country dwelling served to house the entire establishment, classrooms and living quarters for the students and the schoolmistress. Toughkenamon School earned a reputation for its scholastic standards but, like other similar institutions, did not last beyond the lifetime of its founder.

ALLEN FLITCRAFT'S SCHOOL

WOODSTOWN-PILESGROVE LIBRARY

Thaddeus K. Kenderdine, a journalist in later life, perpetuated in his writing his experience at the Quaker boarding school he attended at Eldridge's Hill near Woodstown, N. J. in 1855. Classes were held in the Flitcraft home, where the wife of the schoolmaster cooked and served all the meals. Thirty boys slept two to a bed, dormitory style in a drafty adjoining frame building which had formerly been the village store and postoffice. Twice a week the students marched to Meeting for Worship in Woodstown.

TWO SCHOOLS AND THEIR REAL ESTATE

Abington Friends School

John Barnes, a Philadelphia Friend, in 1697 gave 120 acres of farm land to be used for a meeting house and school in Abington Township. The first building put up on his land in 1702 was used both as a meeting house and school room. A school house was erected in 1784, a two-story affair with one room upstairs and one down. This accommodated the entire school until 1887, when Abington Meeting opened a boarding school which continued only some 25 years. Today Abington Friends School has grades from nursery school through high school.

Abington Meeting and Abington School still own about three-quarters of the land received from John Barnes in 1697. Since it lies at the intersection of Old York Road and Washington Lane in modern Jenkintown, it has become extremely valuable. Old York Road Country Club once leased the property and maintained an 18-hole golf course there until suburban real estate development made it too costly. Now the ground is under 50-year lease to a commercial developer who has placed on it a Lord and Taylor retail store, a large apartment house and the office building-shopping complex called Fox Pavilion.

The buildings will revert to Abington Friends at termination of the lease. Meanwhile, income received by the nine Abington Meeting members who serve as trustees of the Barnes estate, is adjustable in accordance with changes in the cost of living index. The income has already made it much easier to finance new buildings for the school.

Both these buildings are on land acquired in 1687 and still owned by Abington Meeting.

H. THOMAS HALLOWELL, JR.

Friends Select School

Friends Select School in Philadelphia, so called because originally it accepted only Friends as students, was opened in 1833, but had no home of its own for fifty years. Classes were held in meeting houses and in rented properties until 1886, when the school was finally permitted to take over the full city block bounded by Sixteenth, Seventeenth, Cherry and Race Streets which for two hundred years had been a Quaker burying ground. This provided a fine location, only a block from Friends' Central School and only five or six blocks from Penn Charter. Generations later, however, all three schools encountered the same difficulties—outmoded buildings with no room to expand. The others moved to the suburbs and became country day schools, but the school committee for Friends Select worked out a different solution and remained committed to center-city.

After long and complex negotiations, while retaining ownership of the land, Friends executed a lease permitting construction of the 20-story Pennwalt Company office building on half of the block facing Cherry Street and the Parkway. Revenue from the building is adjustable depending upon its

Friends burying gound, 1886.

current rent schedules. After 100 years, the school will own the office building.

To complete the project, Friends placed a mortgage on the ground under Pennwalt's Building, and thus were able to finance a new two-story home for the school on the Race street side of the original lot, still with a front entrance facing the Parkway. The new school occupies about half as much ground as formerly, but now has much more classroom space plus a swimming pool in the basement and playing fields with artificial turf on the roof.

Friends Select School, 1887—1967.

Old School yard and tennis courts.

Friends Select School, 1981.

THREE QUAKER-FOUNDED COLLEGES

Three colleges which rank among the nation's highest for academic excellence—Haverford, Swarthmore and Bryn Mawr—were all founded by Friends. The Quakers were late, however, in recognizing their need for institutions of higher learning. Although they emphasized good schools for their children, they believed at first that colleges were mostly for training the clergymen of other religious organizations.

HAVERFORD

Haverford College was established in 1833 by the Yearly Meeting of Orthodox Friends. After the Great Separation, a series of articles in *The Friend* protested the ultra-conservative view of some Friends that even classical literature was un-Christian. It was proposed to establish "an institution in which the children of Friends shall receive a liberal education in ancient and modern literature and mathematics and natural sciences under the care of competent instructors of our own Society, so as not to endanger their religious principles or alienate them from their early attachment."

Funds were raised by subscription and a charter

obtained for "The Haverford School Association". Founders Hall, begun in 1832, accommodated the entire institution with its opening class of 21 men. The location on a farm near a station of the new Pennsylvania Railroad was chosen both for its rural neighborhood and "a surrounding population remarkable for sobriety."

Haverford in recent years has permitted women students, particularly those from nearby Bryn Mawr, to attend some classes. For the academic year 1980-81, women were admitted for the first time as full-time members of the freshman class.

Haverford College, 1833.

Co-educational Haverford, 1980.

RUFUS M. JONES

Many notable educators have contributed to the success of Quaker schools and left an imprint of Quakerism upon thousands of students, non-Friends as well as Friends. Haverford's Rufus M. Jones was one who also influenced the Society of Friends itself and broadened its mission.

A Haverford graduate, he returned to the college at the age of 30 to teach philosophy, retired after 41 years, then remained as Emeritus Professor and campus resident until his death at 85. "I am happiest when teaching a class of youth," he said. Yet he became a leader in Quaker affairs, too, principal organizer of the American Friends Service Committee and its guiding spirit all his lifetime. He helped join Yearly Meetings in scattered sections of the country into the Five Years Meeting. He was a leading spirit in the movement which eventually brought unity to the two Philadelphia Yearly Meetings.

Swarthmore's "Inauguration," 1869.

Swarthmore Centennial Commencement.

SWARTHMORE

Friends of the Hicksite Meeting were no more comfortable about sending sons to Haverford than that institution was about having them. But it was 1864 before their college, Swarthmore, could be founded. Two Friends from Baltimore Meeting, Martha E. Tyson and Benjamin Hallowell, Jr., initiated the proposal which was finally successful through the combined efforts of Baltimore, Philadelphia and New York Yearly Meetings. Friends of all three Meetings subscribed the funds, and again a farm was chosen as the location—this time a farm at Westdale in Delaware County, Pa. The college was named Swarthmore for Swarthmoor Hall in England where George Fox lived late in life.

Swarthmore opened its doors in 1869 with 82 women students and 88 men, and the college has been co-educational ever since. Women were appointed to the faculty, too, one of the earliest being the redoubtable Susan J. Cunningham, Professor of Mathematics and Astronomy. The first President of Swarthmore was Edward Parrish for whom the original campus building is named. It now serves as administrative headquarters.

At the lectern, Board Chairman Claude C. Smith; in the front row, Lyndon B. Johnson, President of the United States; Swarthmore President Courtney C. Smith; U Thant, Secretary General of the United Nations.

Parrish Hall.

Dr. Joseph W. Taylor.

Taylor Hall.   BRYN MAWR COLLEGE ARCHIVES

BRYN MAWR

Bryn Mawr College came into existence not under the care of any organized Friends Meeting but as fulfillment of the dream of one man, the Quaker physician, Joseph Wright Taylor, of Burlington.

Having had 20 years experience on the Board of Haverford College, Dr. Taylor decided to devote his wealth to creation of a women's college where standards would be the highest. He personally purchased the hilltop site of 39 acres in Bryn Mawr, not far from Haverford, and paid for construction of the first college building. He did not live to see the college open, but his will provided for its organization and left his entire estate for its endowment. The will named Bryn Mawr's first Trustees. Dr. Taylor's friend, James E. Rhoads, also a Quaker physician and member of Haverford's Board, was picked to be the first President.

THE GREAT MEETING HOUSE

PAUL BRUTON

Friends called their first large place of worship in Philadelphia "The Great Meeting House." Built in 1695, it stood on the southwest corner of Second and High Streets. When the City built its court-house there in 1707, with sheds extending down the middle of the street beyond for farmers to sell their produce, High Street became Market Street.

The Great Meeting House was rebuilt and en-larged on the same site in 1755. It was the principal place of Quaker worship during the Revolution and the Presidency of George Washington. But by 1800, the neighborhood had become too busy and too noisy for silent meeting. Friends moved to a new meeting house at Fourth and Arch Streets on ground that William Penn had given the Meeting a century before.

GEORGE VAUX

Before selling the property at Second and Market, Friends moved much of the building material of the Great Meeting House to Twelfth Street and used it in constructing a new meeting house there for the Western District of Philadelphia Monthly Meeting. The salvaged material included huge roof trusses with one-piece wooden beams 55 feet long. Twelfth Street Meeting was completed in 1812 and was a focus of Quaker activity in Philadelphia for the next 150 years. This photo was made before the old building of Penn Charter School was torn down for the towering office building of the Philadelphia Saving Fund Society.

In the commercial shopping district of the 1970s, Twelfth Street Meeting House was no longer needed, with Race Street and Arch Street Meetings now united. Demolition seemed to be the next step, but Friends with a feeling for history came up with a better solution. George School, the Quaker boarding academy in Bucks County, was thinking of building a campus meeting house. Might the historic Philadelphia building be moved there instead? Architectural studies determined it was possible. A generous family interested in Friends education provided the necessary funds.

Twelfth Street Meeting House was carefully taken apart brick by brick and timber by timber. The giant roof trusses made two centuries before for Second and Market Streets were lifted out and transported thirty-five miles by motorcade to George School at 5 A.M. one morning. There were only inches of clearance under the railroad bridge on Highway 413.

Since 1974 the Twelfth Street Meeting House has had a new home on the sweeping campus at George School. Displayed on the north wall inside is a memento of the building's eventful past—a floor joist on which the carpenter Abraham Carlisle and his apprentice used nails to record their initials and the date 1755. Originally the board went into the Great Meeting House when it was rebuilt. It was used again at Twelfth Street and now, after two centuries of service, has been retired.

MEETINGS AND MEETING HOUSES

Philadelphia Yearly Meeting, 1980.

Friends of Salem, N.J. celebrate an anniversary of the founding of their Meeting in 1676.

Men's Yearly Meeting, Race Street, 1924. A message is received from Women's Meeting.

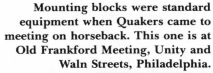

Mounting blocks were standard equipment when Quakers came to meeting on horseback. This one is at Old Frankford Meeting, Unity and Waln Streets, Philadelphia.

A far-from-typical Quaker Meeting House, built in 1873, stood for half a century on Powelton Avenue in West Philadelphia.

Stoves were close to benches in old-time meeting houses. Fans came in handy, too. (Left to right) Woodstown, N.J.; Radnor,Pa., and Falsington, Pa.

When new brick meeting houses were built, the old log or frame ones often became shelters for horses or carriages. This was once the original meeting house at Centreville, Delaware.

Changing styles in Quaker dress: Yearly Meeting, 1905, and Yearly Meeting, 1980.

ATLANTIC CITY HOTEL-KEEPERS

Most of the major hotels of Atlantic City were owned and operated by Quakers from the very beginning of the resort until the era of motels and gambling casinos.

CHALFONTE AND SHELBURNE

Elisha and Elizabeth Hooton Roberts from Mount Holly, who had managed the guest farmhouse at West-town School, moved to Atlantic City in its earliest years and built on North Carolina Avenue "a new and commodious first class boarding house . . . beautifully situated in full view of the ocean." They called it Chalfonte House, and provided a mule car to carry bathers from the hotel over the sand dunes to the water's edge.

Elisha managed the business affairs, Elizabeth supervised the kitchen and dining room while Elizabeth's sister took charge of housekeeping. The Roberts lived in two rooms next to the hotel office. Two of their children were born during that time.

In 1869, the Roberts opened a second "cottage", the Shelburne. It became quite popular with theatrical folk from New York, and Diamond Jim Brady was said to have been a regular guest. Around 1904, the Roberts sold their properties and retired from the hotel business.

Elisha and Elizabeth Roberts.　　　MAY ROBERTS TAYLOR

Leeds and Lippincott.

ALEXANDER J. WILLIAMSON

THE DENNIS

The headmaster of Burlington Friends School, William Dennis, built a family cottage on Michigan Avenue in 1860 and gradually expanded it into a 22-room boarding house. He sold it to another Burlington Quaker, Joseph H. Borton, who built a full-size hotel and named it The Dennis. A third Friend, Walter J. Buzby, purchased the property at the turn of the century and built it into one of the resort's best-known. Buzby and his sons operated the Dennis until its sale in 1970.

HADDON HALL

Friends from Riverton, Sarah West Leeds and her husband, Samuel, moved to Belmar, New Jersey, because of his health. Six buildings from the Centennial Exposition of 1876 had been moved to the beach there and converted into boarding houses. When Sarah West undertook to manage one of them, she discovered her talents as business executive and hostess.

The Leeds' 22-year-old son, Henry West Leeds, decided he would like to enter the hotel business. He formed a partnership with his life-long companion, J. Haines Lippincott, who had just left Swarthmore College, and persuaded his mother to move to Atlantic City to advise them. They bought a place which Samuel and Susanna Wheaton Hunt, of Haddonfield, had built twenty years before and had named, naturally, the Haddon House. The two young men learned hotel-keeping under the guidance of "Mother Sarah."

The venture prospered from the beginning. In 1900 the partners bought the Chalfonte, just across North Carolina Avenue, and built four years later a new ten-story building, the first fireproof hotel in the resort. Chalfonte-Haddon Hall became Atlantic City's largest, remaining under the management of Henry Leeds and Haines Lippincott and their sons until sold to become the first legalized casino.

MARLBOROUGH—BLENHEIM

Quaker Josiah White, III bought his first hotel, the Lurray, in 1887, only to have it burn not long after. He then built the Marlborough on the beachfront at Ohio Avenue. When an amusement park across the street installed a roller coaster almost under the windows of his guests, he bought that property too, and erected the Blenheim, with a bridge to connect it with the Marlborough. The Blenheim was the first of Atlantic City's hotels to provide a private bath with every room. It was built of reinforced concrete mixed in accordance with specifications provided by Thomas A. Edison.

THE TRAYMORE

A ten-room boarding house named the Traymore was purchased by Daniel S. White, still another Quaker, in 1870 and transformed by 1900 into the largest hotel in Atlantic City at that time. It was the first to be equipped with elevators. It remained in the hands of the White family until the 1970s.

OTHER QUAKER HOTELS

Nathan Leeds Jones, from Moorestown, owned and operated the Glaslyn-Chatham, on Park Avenue, for upwards of thirty years. Ezra T. Bell and Paul M. Cope, the latter a Clerk of Atlantic City Friends Meeting, conducted the Morton Hotel. The Seaside, one of the largest Quaker-built hotels, was put up in 1862 by David Scattergood and sold three years later to the partnership of Charles Evans and Caspar Wistar Haines. It passed out of Friends ownership, however, in 1903.

HOTELMEN AND TEACHERS

Quaker hotel-keepers were mainstays of the Atlantic City Friends Meeting and the Friends School. During the Great Depression of the 1930s, the situation at the seashore became so bad, the school teachers met payless paydays. To help out in this temporary crisis, the hotel owners invited the teachers to take meals in their dining rooms. It helped the teachers, and gave the hotels the appearance of being busy, which they weren't.

Old Atlantic City Meeting House.

The Giant Sequoia.
This great tree grows close beside Painter Road. The upper portion has a double trunk because someone in search of an unusually attractive Christmas tree cut out the top of it in 1895. Fortunately, the twin trunks have grown together and the shape of this handsome giant has not been spoiled.

A giant sequoia, a tree native only to the Sierra Nevada of California, is growing in Delaware County, Pennsylvania, and has been growing there for 125 years.

Two remarkable Quaker brothers, Minshall and Jacob Painter, planted this horticultural rarity (not to be confused with a California redwood) a few years before the Civil War on land their ancestors obtained in Pennsylvania's earliest days. They collected many other fine specimens on the farm near Media which never passed out of the family and has now become the John J. Tyler Arboretum.

Minshall Painter, born in 1801, eldest of seven children, and Jacob, born 1814, the youngest, were born on the place, called Latchford Hall for the ancestral home in England. They lived there all their lives, never married and died there in 1870s. They were men of comfortable circumstances, not dependent upon the farm for a living, able to devote time and attention to simple and scholarly enjoyments.

The older brother was a skilled mechanic, able to make almost anything out of wood or metal, and a born natural scientist. He studied and collected plants, minerals and insects, made observations of the stars and kept detailed meteorological records. Jacob was a lover of books, a writer of poetry as well as papers on philosophy, ethics and Quakerism. He invented his own system of library classification.

The brothers were not travellers, but they gathered trees, shrubs, small plants and flowers from the nation over, caring for them in the well-maintained garden and arboretum of Latchford Hall. Close by their house they built a small, two-story stone library for their collection of more than a thousand volumes of scholarly nature. The building had open passages from the basement upwards through the thick walls, providing an ingenious system for cooling and humidifying. The library contained the press on which they printed articles on whatever subjects were currently of interest to them, not as a commercial venture but a means of sharing their observations with friends and neighbors.

When both brothers had died, the Painter property passed to their sister, Anne Painter Tyler, and then to her nephew, John J. Tyler, a Philadelphian who occupied Latchford Hall as a summer residence. He and his wife, Laura Hoopes Tyler, established the Tyler Arboretum and provided its endowment. The public is welcomed to enjoy not only the plants and the grounds, but also to view the library and the house which remains furnished with family belongings much as it was when the Painter brothers lived there.

FRIENDS BOARDING HOMES

Concern for welfare of the elderly led to the introduction of a new type of Friends Boarding Home in the 1890s. Most of them were operated under the care of Quarterly Meetings. They sought to provide "an abiding place where at moderate terms, all the needful home comforts may be obtained."

Nine Boarding Homes are still maintained for Friends "and those in sympathy with us." The Home of Concord Quarterly Meeting in West Chester dates back to 1891. Its original building, Old Main, has been renovated to remain in service beside the modern Hickman Memorial Building. In Chester County also are the Barclay in West Chester, and Friends Home of Western Quarter in Kennett Square.

The Philadelphia Home is Stapeley Hall in Germantown. The Bucks Quarter has a Home in Newtown, and The Harned is in Moylan, Delaware County. Three of the Homes are in New Jersey: Friends Home at Woodstown, the Greenleaf in Moorestown, and Penlyn in Trenton.

Friends Boarding Home of Concord.

Kennett Square.

Newtown.

Woodstown.

ANNA T. JEANES AND STAPELEY HALL

Friends Boarding Home in Philadelphia, Stapeley Hall, is a living memorial to Anna T. Jeanes, an old-fashioned Quaker lady and generous benefactor of many Friends institutions and programs.

In 1895, at the very time that Philadelphia Friends in Yearly Meeting were wrestling with the problem of providing Homes for older Friends, deaths in her family left Anna Jeanes, age 72, living alone in the family townhouse in the once-fashionable neighborhood of Tenth and Arch Streets. She was such a modest and retiring person that few members of Meeting knew her, but she was well acquainted with what they were planning. When the Committee came back the next year to recommend development of Friends Boarding Homes, Anna Jeanes unexpectedly sent in a check for $200,000 to help.

When Friends established a boarding home in Germantown, Philadelphia, Anna Jeanes became a resident, leaving her town house in the possession of family servants. She decided, however, that the building was not well suited to the purpose, so at her own expense, she purchased a four-acre lot at the corner of Washington Lane and Greene Street and built Stapeley Hall, naming it for the Jeanes family's country place.

A newpaper of the time says: "the aged woman conducted the operation in person, employing the architects and builders and conferring with them over every detail, large or small. Several times weekly, she visited the building, taking active part in the supervision of the work." Upon completion, she turned the entire property over to the Meeting, moved in as one of the residents and lived there until her death in 1907.

Anna T. Jeanes.
No life-time portrait is known to exist. This painting which hangs in the lobby of Stapeley Hall was executed after her death by one of her fellow residents. It was regarded by those who knew her as an accurate portrayal not only of her appearance, but also her old-fashioned Quaker manner.

The story is that she came to the conclusion that Stapeley Hall needed a large garden in which the Home could raise vegetables and residents would be able to cultivate flowers. One of Philadelphia's richest bankers owned four adjoining acres, but did not want to sell it. Anna Jeanes sent a friend to press the matter. The owner did not want to offend the elderly ladies in the Home by an outright refusal of their request. Instead, he fixed an outrageously high price which he thought would end the matter. Anna Jeanes sent him a check, and Stapeley Hall acquired additional room for lawns and gardens.

Anna Jeanes made other gifts of $100,000 and $200,000 to Friends Meeting for the support of Quaker schools, for the maintenance of meeting houses in smaller communities and for the support of needy Friends living in Quaker boarding houses. Although she specified preference for Friends, her benefactions often read "for Friends or those in sympathy with us." Her largest life-time gift was $1,000,000 to Booker T. Washington and his associates for the support of schools for black children in the rural South.

In her will, Anna Jeanes left bequests to a number of her fellow residents in Stapeley Hall and to the Home itself. She benefitted dozens of charitable organizations, Friends as well as non-Quaker. The bulk of her estate went to Yearly Meeting to build and endow Jeanes Hospital, now a general hospital located on what was once the Jeanes family farm in Foxchase.

The renowned Longwood Gardens near Kennett Square, Pennsylvania, include land which was deeded by William Penn to George Peirce, one of his Quaker settlers, in 1684.

Peirce's son built this substantial brick farmhouse on the property in 1730. Two generations later, twin great-grandsons Joshua and Samuel Peirce, interested in natural sciences, and especially botany, began collecting unusual trees and shrubs, planting them around the homestead. In 1849 a noted horticulturist wrote:

"The brothers Joshua and Samuel Peirce have produced an arboretum of evergreens and other elegant forest trees which is certainly unrivalled in Pennsylvania and probably not surpassed in these United States."

For generations, the arboretum and two small lakes on the farm were always open to neighbors in the Kennett Square area. The property became known as "Peirce's Park", a popular spot for picnics and outdoor recreation. In 1899, however, the land passed out of the Peirce family and in 1906 the neighborhood learned the new owners had contracted with a Lancaster lumber company for cutting its finest trees. This news reached a young engineer courting a girl in Kennett Square. He was then doing some work for Pierre S. duPont in Wilmington and told duPont about the situation. Within a few days duPont had purchased the old Peirce property and bought out the lumber contract, the beginning of Longwood Gardens.

The name Longwood came from one of several adjoining farms acquired by duPont after he began to develop Peirce's Park into its modern form. It became his principal hobby and recreation for the rest of his life. Since his home and office were in Wilmington, only twelve miles away, Longwood was his favorite spot for relaxation and enjoyment. He modernized the old Peirce farmhouse, adding a conservatory and a new guest wing with a large ballroom for parties. He and his wife themselves used the original part of the house, converting the old kitchen with its huge fireplace into their dining room.

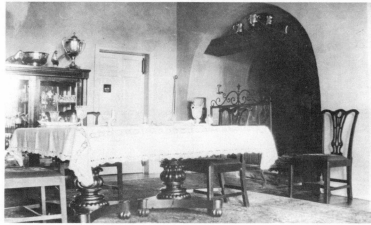

The 1730 Peirce dwelling now houses administrative offices of Longwood Gardens. The old portions of the farmhouse and the ancient Peirce trees are among the many attractions which draw tens of thousands of visitors to the Gardens every year.

QUAKER GOLFERS

The Ozone Club at Northfield Country Club.

Four clubs of Quakers in the Philadelphia area meet about once a month to play a round of golf and to enjoy lunch or dinner together. It has been going on since 1901.

Henry Leeds proposed the idea of "A Friends Golf Union" soon after he became a hotelman in Atlantic City at a time when first steps were being taken to bring the two groups of Friends together. At his suggestion, Walter P. Stokes, James G. Biddle and Joseph H. Roberts invited twenty men belonging to various Friends Meetings to be overnight guests at Haddon Hall and to play 36 holes of golf on January 16, 1901 at Northfield Country Club.

In those days before air pollution was a topic of conversation, ozone was regarded as a bracing element of the great outdoors. Leeds' guests christened their group the Ozone Club, and the name is retained still. At the end of the season, a first annual meeting was held at Haddon Hall with members and their wives guests of the hotel for the week-end. In later years, other Quaker hotelmen became members and their houses competed with each other providing hospitality for the golfers in the off-season.

Ozone Club in 1981 consists of thirty men. Some are senior citizens, some in their thirties; some are men of prominence and wealth, some in modest circumstances; some play golf in the 70s and 80s, while others are likely to shoot 110 or as much as 125.

After World War I, again at Leeds' suggestion, two additional men's clubs were organized—The Divotees and the Niblicks—and a Quaker women's group was formed principally of wives and daughters of members of the others. The lady golfers chose the name Hit or Miss Club.

First match of the Niblicks, 1923.

A Friendly Foursome.
J. Haines Lippincott, Walter J. Buzby, Benjamin Thorp, Henry, W. Leeds.

Annual Meeting of the Divotees, 1961.

Annual Dinner of Ozone Club—1910.

The Hit or Miss Club, 1923.
Rain changed their first match into a
putting contest on the roof garden of Haddon Hall.

"The Quaker Open"—First three-way match, Ozone,
Niblicks and Divotees, Waynesborough, 1980.

Members of Hit or Miss at
Saint Davids Golf Club, 1980.

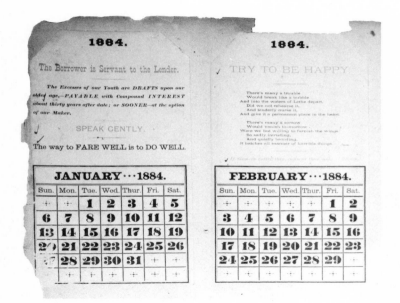

THE QUAKER MOTTO CALENDARS

These plain little red-white-and-blue "Motto Calendars" carry memories for generations of Friends in Philadelphia Yearly Meeting who have seen them appear year after year throughout all their lives. The 1981 calendar is virtually unchanged in appearance and format from the first one distributed in 1884.

Thomas Scattergood, president of a large Philadelphia manufacturing company and descendant of Quakers active in Meeting for many generations, began distributing calendars like these to his employees as his form of personal ministry. Calendars were not then widely used for advertising purposes. Scattergood hoped they would prove both useful and inspirational. For more than 20 years he selected the quotations to be printed on each page and sent out the calendars to an ever-growing list.

Since Scattergood's death in 1907, members of his family have anonymously carried on his project. At one time a million calendars a year were being produced. They are no longer provided free, but are kept available on a minimum cost basis. Those who wish may obtain information through the office of Philadelphia Yearly Meeting.

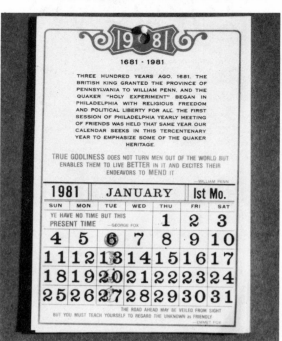

FRIENDS HOSPITAL

ACCOUNT

OF

THE RISE AND PROGRESS

OF

THE ASYLUM,

Proposed to be Established, near Philadelphia,

FOR THE

RELIEF OF PERSONS

DEPRIVED OF THE USE OF THEIR REASON.

WITH AN

ABRIDGED ACCOUNT

OF

THE RETREAT,

A SIMILAR INSTITUTION NEAR YORK IN ENGLAND.

PHILADELPHIA:
PUBLISHED BY KIMBER AND CONRAD,
NO. 93, MARKET STREET.
Merritt, Printer.
1814.

An idea first modestly proposed to Philadelphia Yearly Meeting in 1811 continues as a testimony to the loving concern of Friends for fellow human beings and their innovative spirit in seeking new solutions for old problems.

Persons with mental illness were for centuries confined rather than treated. Often it was felt they must be harshly dealt with in order to drive out demons which possessed them. But English Friends at York pioneered humane and "moral" treatment of insanity at The Retreat established by William Tuke, and a Philadelphian who visited York, Thomas Scattergood, proposed a similar institution for Philadelphia after he returned home. The Yearly Meeting approved the undertaking "for such of our members as may be deprived of the use of their reason."

Friends subscribed the funds needed to buy a farm, erect a building and open "The Friends Asylum" for its first two patients in 1817. It was the first facility in America for treating the mentally ill "as brethren and men" who could be restored to health and productive life.

Friends hospital today is open to all, but still managed by a board of Philadelphia Quakers. The concerns of generations of Friends have made it one of the nation's leading psychiatric hospitals. Its methods of treatment are the most modern of medical science, but its guiding principles are still those of the founders—humane treatment, respect for the individual, the conviction there is "that of God" in everyone.

"Friends"
Presented to Friends Hospital
by the sculptress,
Sylvia Shaw Judson.

115

Friends Hospital still occupies its original site, the 1817 building still in use for clinical and administrative offices, the main entrance on Roosevelt Boulevard directly opposite the Sears Roebuck building.

HORTICULTURAL THERAPY

Since the day it opened, Friends Hospital has emphasized the importance of nature and the outdoors in restoring troubled minds. Acres of its grounds have always been devoted to trees, shrubs and flowers. Large greenhouses have been in existence for a century. Patients are healed while mixing soil, digging and propagating, pruning, arranging and planting.

In contrast to the old concept of dark and dismal asylums for the mentally ill, the grounds of Friends Hospital are open for the enjoyment of patients, families and friends, and the surrounding neighborhood. Tens of thousands visit every Spring to see the almost unbelievable displays of azaleas and other blossoms.

Main House.

Howard H. Brinton and Anna Cox Brinton, who came from the academic world to be co-directors of Pendle Hill, 1936-1952.

Named for "the great hill" where George Fox said "the Lord let me see in what places he had a great people to be gathered", Pendle Hill is a unique combination of educational institution and Quaker religious retreat. It has a pleasing campus of 22 acres in Wallingford, Pennsylvania, not far from Swarthmore College.

Pendle Hill is officially described as "a Quaker center for study and contemplation". Since Friends have no professional ministry, it can also be considered a seminary for Quaker leaders. And at times it has been called a Quaker monastery.

Half the Pendle Hill community is year-round staff, the other half students ranging in age from senior citizens to teen-agers, sometimes with young children, and "sojourners" who come to spend a day or a week in the atmosphere of the campus. Courses include religious thought, Quaker-

ism, Bible study, social action and literature. Daily meetings for worship are part of the schedule. Housekeeping and outdoor maintenance work are shared by all.

Pendle Hill celebrated its 50th anniversary in 1980.

A one-time barn was been converted into a lecture hall and meeting room for Quaker worship.

Classes are informal and often held outdoors. Kitchen duty is shared by all.

FRIENDS RETIREMENT COMMUNITIES

Quakers of the Philadelphia area have become leading organizers and managers of modern non-profit retirement communities which provide both independent living for active older people and lifetime medical care for those requiring it.

Six such communities opened by Friends in a dozen years have proved so successful they are used as models in other sections of the country. Some have waiting lists long enough to fill them for years to come, a majority of residents as well as applicants being non-Friends.

FOULKEWAYS

The history of the first community, Foulkeways, began after a large farm across the road from Gwynedd Meeting House was left to the Meeting under the will of Charles O. Beaumont as a memorial to his wife, the former May Foulke. Neither he nor she was a Friend, but May Foulke had always wanted the Meeting to have the farm. It had belonged to her Quaker grandfather. It was her favorite summer retreat in earlier years and her year-round home after she became an invalid.

When Foulkeways opened in 1967, the first resident to enroll was Eliza Ambler Foulke, still an active member of Gwynedd Meeting. She is a direct descendant of Edward and Eleanor Foulke, the first of the family in America. She has presented to Foulkeways the original William Penn deed conveying to them in 1698 the Foulke ancestral home in Penllyn, about five miles from Gwynedd.

DONALD M. STEELE

Foulkeways, Gwynedd, Pa.

Pennswood Village, 1980

The newest of Friends retirement communities is on the campus at George School, Newtown, Pa.

KENDAL AND CROSSLANDS

Two years after its opening, Kendal-at-Longwood had accumulated such a long waiting list its Board offered to build another community, Crosslands, on a different site and to have it ready for occupancy in September, 1977, if enough of those on the list would agree to move into it at that time and would deposit one half of the purchase price in advance. The proposal was readily accepted. Crosslands was "full" before the Quaker Board of Directors even bought the land. Construction was completed on time. All occupants of the 250 apartments and cottages moved in during the month which had been designated two years before.

Like Foulkeways, the Crosslands property has its own bit of Quaker history. The land was owned continuously by the Webb-Savery family from the beginning of Pennsylvania until the sale to Crosslands.

"Ellerslie", now the guest house for overnight visitors and private parties given by Crosslands residents, was built in 1827. It was intended by the Webbs as a wedding present for their son, Ellis, and the girl he was soon to marry. But 1827 was the year of "The Great Separation". When Kennett Meeting divided, the family of the bride-to-be remained with the Hicksite group in the old Kennett Meeting House. The Webbs withdrew to help organize the Orthodox Parkersville Meeting. The wedding was called off, and Ellis Webb never married. The house eventually became the property of his sister, Hannah Harvey Webb, when she married Thomas Savery.

Kendal-at-Longwood.
Opened 1973 near Longwood Gardens, Pa.

GEORGE A. KNOWLES

"Ellerslie", built in 1827.

WILFRED H. WICKERSHAM

RUTH E. BONNER

Crosslands.

Medford Leas. Opened 1972 at Medford, N. J.

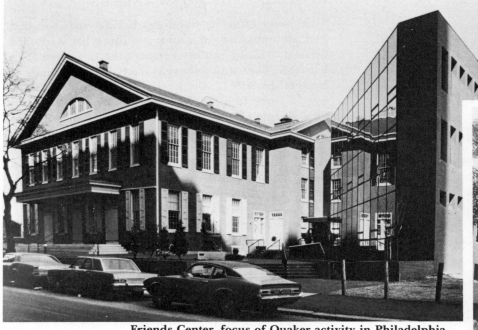

Friends Center, focus of Quaker activity in Philadelphia.
A dramatic glass wall of the new office building reflects
the adjoining meeting house dating back to 1856.

FRIENDS CENTER, PHILADELPHIA

Philadelphia Yearly Meeting still holds its annual sessions in the 1804 meeting house at Fourth and Arch Streets, but the main center of every-day Quaker activity in Philadelphia is now the new Friends Center at Fifteenth, Race and Cherry Streets. Here the meeting house built in 1856 is now adjoined by a modern brick office building which, without interfering with its historic neighbor, forms an integrated working complex with it.

This is the administrative headquarters for the Yearly Meeting and its working committees as well as half a dozen Quaker organizations of national

and international scope which are based in Philadelphia. Among these are the American Friends Service Committee; Friends World Committee for Consultation (Section of the Americas); Friends General Conference; Friends Council on Education; and the publication, *Friends Journal.*

Housed here also is the Central Philadelphia Monthly Meeting. The entire Friends Center complex is owned and maintained by Friends Center Corporation, a unique joint venture of the Yearly Meeting, the Monthly Meeting and the American Friends Service Committee.

Facilities at Friends Center
include the Yearly Meeting
Library and the Friends Bookstore.

Meeting for Worship on the beach at Cape May, N.J., long a feature of summer gatherings of Friends General Conference.

FRIENDS GENERAL CONFERENCE

In the Society of Friends, each Yearly Meeting is autonomous. There is no central hierarchy or administrative authority comparable to those of other religious organizations. In order to keep the Yearly Meetings in touch with each other, several loosely-organized associations have come into existence.

Friends General Conference, organized in 1900 and based in Philadelphia, is the oldest of these associations. Philadelphia Yearly Meeting is one of thirteen Yearly Meetings affiliated with it. For many years Friends General Conference sponsored the biennial summer gatherings at Cape May, N.J. attended by hundreds of Friends and their families. Since 1963, these summer sessions have been scheduled annually, alternating between the east

coast and the mid-west at such places as Ithaca College, New York; Earlham College, Indiana; and Berea College, Kentucky.

Generally similar to Friends General Conference are three other associations: Friends United Meeting (formerly the Five Years Meeting), based in Indiana; the Evangelical Friends Alliance; and Conservative Friends. With a few exceptions, Yearly Meetings attached to Friends General Conference and Conservative Friends follow the traditional style of silent, unprogrammed Quaker worship. Most of those associated with Friends United Meeting and the Evangelical Friends are pastoral meetings with programmed worship.

AMERICAN FRIENDS SERVICE COMMITTEE

The one Quaker activity best known by most people who are not Friends is the work of the American Friends Service Committee. For more than 60 years it has been helping relieve suffering and human misery wherever found.

When organized in Philadelphia at the outbreak of World War I, A.F.S.C. was described as "a service of love in wartime." A minute of the first meeting said: "We are united in expressing our love for our country and our desire to serve her loyally. We offer our service to the Government in any constructive way in which we can conscientiously serve humanity." The first programs were rebuilding war-ravaged villages in France and feeding children in Germany after the conflict.

At home and in many lands, the Service Committee has provided food, clothing and shelter for the needy, furnished medicine and medical care, tried to improve living conditions for the destitute, worked for peace among individuals and among nations. Hundreds of volunteers donate their services to augment the efforts of the staff.

Philadelphia is still world-wide headquarters, but A.F.S.C. is by no means only a Philadelphia institution. Regional offices are maintained in ten other cities from Massachusetts to California. Financial support comes from Friends Meetings and individual Friends throughout the country. By far the majority of A.F.S.C. financial support, however, comes from those who are not Friends but who place their trust in its very practical demonstration of Quaker beliefs and principles.

Clarence Pickett
A.F.S.C. Executive Director, 1929-1950.

World War I: feeding German children, reconstruction in France, care for French orphans.

Headquarters Staff at
Twelfth Street Meeting, 1937.

Young Friends Peace Caravan, 1930.

Milk for coal miners' children, Kentucky, 1931.

Rebuilding a bombed out Italian
mountain village, World War II.

A.F.S.C.'s Chairman, Henry J. Cadbury, accepts the 1947 Nobel Peace Prize
awarded jointly to American and British Friends.

A.F.S.C.—"A SERVICE OF LOVE"

Aid for a crippled boy in Vietnam in the 1960s.

Food and medicine for refugees in Cambodia, 1979.

Quaker House, New York City—A quiet retreat where United Nations delegates, staff and families can meet, talk and dine together as friends, 1981.

A QUAKER COMMUNITY

It is hard to spend more than a day in the territory of Philadelphia Yearly Meeting without coming into contact with at least one well-known institution, business enterprise or civic improvement project started years ago by a Quaker man or woman and still serving the generations of today. This tercentenary album has space for only a few examples.

WILLS EYE HOSPITAL

One of the world's foremost institutions specializing in eye care, Wills Eye Hospital in Philadelphia, came into existence under the will of James Wills, Jr., a Philadelphia Quaker who died in 1825.

Wills was the son of a Friend who emigrated from England and worked at first as driver and man-of-all-work for the family of Anthony Benezet, Quaker schoolmaster. Later in life he opened a grocery in Philadelphia. James Wills, Jr., born in 1777, entered his father's business and ultimately accumulated a sizeable estate. When he died unmarried at 48, he made several charitable bequests including $5000 to Friends Hospital, and left the bulk of his property to "The Mayor and Corporation of the City of Philadelphia" to purchase land to build "a hospital or asylum to be denominated The Wills Hospital for the relief of the indigent, blind and lame".

The hospital was situated for a century on Logan Square, then moved in 1930 to Seventeenth and Spring Garden Streets. Last year, after affiliation with Thomas Jefferson University, Wills Eye Hospital completed and occupied a new $26,000,000 building at Ninth and Walnut Streets close to Jefferson Hospital.

WILLS EYE HOSPITAL

Wills Hospital about 1890.

OBITUARY.

DIED, suddenly, on the evening of the 22d. inst. JAMES WILLS, Grocer, in the 48th. year of his age.

His friends are respectfully invited to attend the burial, from his late residence, No. 84 Chesnut-street, this afternoon, at half past two o'clock.

LIBRARY COMPANY OF PHILADELPHIA

WILLIAM BANCROFT AND THE WOODLAWN TRUSTEES

The park system and excellent residential suburbs of Wilmington, Delaware, are owed primarily to one man, William Poole Bancroft. Son of the founder of the old Bancroft Cotton Mills on the Brandywine, he earned in the business the means to support generously many Quaker and community projects, but his principal interest was constructive city planning for Wilmington and preservation of the beautiful Brandywine Valley.

Bancroft was instrumental in forming the Wilmington Park Commission, was its President nearly twenty years, presented it with over 200 acres of land for park purposes and aided it in the acquisition of additional acreage at reasonable cost. He created the Woodlawn Company, later Woodlawn Trustees, Inc., to carry out his work after his lifetime. A section of Wilmington was developed as a model residential area. Low rental housing was built in several sections. Large holdings of land in the valley have been purchased for gradual development consistent with healthy and attractive environment for residents. Bancroft died in 1928, but his plans are still being carried out.

William P. Bancroft.

FAIRMOUNT PARK

Philadelphia's great Fairmount Park, 4000 acres of open space inside the city, consisted originally of only a small space surrounding the municipal reservoir on "Faire Mount", the hill where the Art Museum is now placed.

Expansion of the Park began in 1843 when Thomas P. Cope, a Quaker merchant and ship-owner, led a campaign in City Council to acquire the adjoining 52 acre estate, Lemon Hill. As chairman of a Council committee, he succeeded in purchasing for the City for $75,000 a property which some years before had sold for $225,000. In 1854, after their father's death, Cope's sons, Alfred and Thomas, organized a group of contributors who bought another estate, Sedgeley, and turned it over to the City at a reduced price, extending the park to Girard Avenue.

Cedar Grove, a Quaker country house build in Frankford in 1721, now stands in West Fairmount Park near Memorial Hall. Lydia Thompson Morris gave it to the Park in 1927 along with the furniture and furnishings assembled by her family over more than 200 years.

Thomas P. Cope.

Jesse George.

Lemon Hill.

GEORGES' HILL

Another magnificent addition to the Park came in 1883 when the elderly brother and sister, Jesse and Rebecca George, made an outright gift of 82 acres which had been owned in their family since the founding of Pennsylvania. They were cousins of John M. George, whose bequest established George School.

The Jesse and Rebecca George property was well west of the area which City Council had hoped might someday become part of the Park. It lay directly in the path of residential development in West Philadelphia, growing more and more valuable every year. But the two Quaker owners deeded it to the city "for the health, recreation and enjoyment of the citizens of Philadelphia." An overwhelmed City Council decreed that the lofty hill rising at the western end of the property should be forever known as Georges' Hill.

The Philadelphia Orchestra now plays summer concerts on Georges' Hill overlooking the city skyline.

AMERICA'S OLDEST BUSINESS

The Marple Homestead. The business was here for 175 years.

Joseph Rhoads opened a tannery on his farm at Marple, twelve miles from Philadelphia in 1702. When he died in 1732, his wife, Abigail ran the business for ten or twelve years until their son, James, was able to take over. His descendants, in turn, operated the business at the family homestead until after the Civil War. To assure themselves a good supply of hides, they paid commissions to tollgate keepers to collect them from farmers making their way to market in Philadelphia.

Jonathan Rhoads, of the fifth generation, moved the tannery to Wilmington and introduced the manufacture of leather belting for industrial plants.

When his sons entered the business, the name was changed to J. E. Rhoads & Sons. Soon after, Jonathan Rhoads retired and devoted himself entirely to Quaker religious concerns.

Today the plant of J. E. Rhoads & Sons, Inc. is in Newark, Delaware. The business has been able to reach the age of 279 years by continually adapting to changes in the business and industrial world. Leather is no longer the company's mainstay. Synthetic fibres and plastics have been developed. But two facts about the old business remain unchanged: it is still owned and operated by Joseph Rhoads' descendants, and they are Friends.

CHEYNEY STATE COLLEGE

Institute for Colored Youth, about 1910.

When Richard Humphreys, Quaker silversmith, died in 1732, his will named 13 members of Philadelphia Monthly Meeting as trustees of a fund he left to establish a school for boys "of African descent." Soon after, the trustees opened The Institute for Colored Youth on a farm on Old York Road. The boys were required to attend Abington Meeting twice a week. It was hoped that the farm would help make the school self-supporting, but that was not the case. The Institute was reorganized and became a free high school for training black teachers. It was located for years on Bainbridge Street near Ninth in Philadelphia.

Around the turn of the century, the trustees of the Institute moved it to a farm at Cheyney, Pa. The first building there, Humphreys Hall, was dedicated in 1905 with the entire student body of nearby Westtown School in attendance. In 1914, the trustees appointed Leslie Pinckney Hill as President of the Institute and shortly thereafter changed its name to Cheyney Training School for Teachers. It became part of the Pennsylvania system of State Colleges in 1922. The Quaker trustees of Humphrey's estate continue to apply its income to help needy students at Cheyney as well as other institutions of higher learning.

STRAWBRIDGE AND CLOTHIER

Justus Clayton Strawbridge.

Isaac Hallowell Clothier.

The business started in 1868 by two young partners, Justus Clayton Strawbridge and Isaac Hallowell Clothier, is still in existence, still occupying its original site at Eighth and Market Streets, Philadelphia, plus 23 other locations. Descendants of the fourth generation are now participating in the management. It is the last major independent department store in the country.

Strawbridge was an Orthodox Friend, Clother a Hicksite. It made little difference except in their loyalty to rival Quaker colleges. Strawbridge supported Haverford and sent his sons there. Clothiers went to Swarthmore, where the Clothier Memorial Building with its lofty Gothic tower is the dominating feature of the campus. Not all descendants have retained membership in the Society of Friends, but the Quakerly "thee" and "thy" are still heard on occasion among family executives.

PENN MUTUAL LIFE INSURANCE COMPANY

PENN MUTUAL LIFE INSURANCE COMPANY

John West Hornor.

John West Hornor, 37-year-old hardware merchant, organized Penn Mutual Life Insurance Company in 1847. He was a Quaker descended from Friends who settled in Bordentown, N. J. in 1683. His original Board of Trustees for the Company did not consist entirely of Quakers, but most of them were. They named the enterprise after Penn, and advertised the soundness of the business by stressing its Quaker virtues. John Hornor held the principal executive position, Secretary, or Clerk, for 26 years. The company's first policy was one written on his life.

A statue of William Penn was mounted over the entrance to Penn Mutual's 1850 building at Third and Dock Streets. When the company moved, Penn was left behind, but in 1947, as part of a centennial celebration, his statue was transferred to a place of honor in the present headquarters on Independence Square.

128

ISAIAH WILLIAMSON'S FREE SCHOOL

Isaiah V. Williamson, 1803-1889.

Williamson Administration Building.

An unusual residential school on a roomy campus near Media, Pa. for almost a century has been providing free vocational education, free housing and free board for about 200 young men who have mechanical aptitudes but whose families cannot afford training beyond high school. Its instruction and its discipline have been so successful that graduates usually have their choice of job offers.

Isaiah V. Williamson, a self-made Quaker merchant, financier and philanthropist, created the Williamson Free School of Mechanical Trades in 1888 with a gift of $2,000,000 and a deed of trust in which he wrote:

"I especially direct that each scholar shall be taught to speak the truth at all times, and I particularly direct and charge as an imperative duty upon the Trustees that each and every scholar shall be thoroughly trained in habits of frugality, economy and industry, as above all others the one great lesson which I desire to have impressed upon every scholar and inmate of the School is that in this country every able-bodied, healthy young man who has learned a good mechanical trade, and is truthful, honest, frugal, temperate and industrious, is certain to succeed in life, and to become a useful and respected member of society."

The Williamson Board of Trustees today consists primarily of graduates who have achieved success in a wide variety of business and industry.

LUKENS STEEL CORPORATION

Today's Lukens Steel Corporation, Coatesville, Pa., takes its name from the young Quaker woman who owned and ran it for more than 20 years—Rebecca Pennock Lukens.

Rebecca's father, Isaac Pennock, founded the Federal Slitting Mill at Rokeby, Chester County, in 1793. Later he acquired the Brandywine Iron Works and Nail Factory which was founded in 1810 by Quaker Jesse Kersey. Dr. Charles Lukens became operator of both plants and husband of Rebecca Pennock. When he died suddenly in 1825, 30-year-old Rebecca—mother of four children and carrying a fifth—had to take his place. She became an Iron-master in her own right and successfully managed the company until 1849 when Charles Huston, husband of her daughter, Isabella, entered the business.

The former Brandywine Iron Works has been called Lukens Iron and Lukens Steel ever since.

Rebecca Pennock Lukens.

THE FEMALE MEDICAL COLLEGE

The Philadelphia County Medical Society issued an official pronouncement in the 1840s declaring that women were "unfit for the profession due to their delicate organization and predominance of the nervous system." Women who wanted to study medicine were barred from medical schools.

A few physicians, most of them Quakers, permitted women as apprentices to learn what they could from observing the doctors' practices. Thereafter, one of the Quaker doctors, Joseph S. Longshore and a Quaker business man, William J. Mullen, obtained a Pennsylvania State Charter in 1850 and founded the Female Medical College of Pennsylvania "to instruct respectable and intelligent females in the various branches of medical science." There were eight students in the first classes held in rented rooms near Seventh and Arch Streets.

Hannah Myers Longshore, wife of Dr. Thomas Longshore, was the first graduate to open practice in Philadelphia. Isaac Barton, a Friend, left the bequest which enabled the college to erect a building of its own on College Avenue in 1868. Dr. Clara Marshall, another Quaker graduate of the college, served as Dean for 29 years. Under her leadership, the college opened its own hospital in 1904, expanded the course of study to four years, and built up a faculty of 60, of whom three-quarters were women.

In 1930, the college and hospital moved to the present location on Henry Avenue. Since 1970, when men students were admitted for the first time, the name of the institution has been Medical College of Pennsylvania.

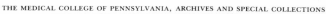
THE MEDICAL COLLEGE OF PENNSYLVANIA, ARCHIVES AND SPECIAL COLLECTIONS

Hannah M. Longshore

Pharmacology Laboratory, 1903

PROVIDENT LIFE AND TRUST COMPANY

PROVIDENT NATIONAL BANK

Samuel R. Shipley.

Nine Philadelphia Friends headed by Samuel R. Shipley organized Provident Life and Trust Company in 1865. Some of them had been in England and studied the business of the Friends Provident Institution of Bedford which wrote policies only on the lives of birthright Friends and enjoyed an extremely low mortality experience. The Philadelphia Quakers didn't go quite that far, but they did announce they were in business to insure only "Friends and others of like careful habits."

Samuel Shipley himself set a good example of longevity, holding the office of President continuously for 41 years before resigning in 1906. By that time the company's two original lines of business, life insurance and banking, had grown quite separate. In 1922 Provident was divided into the two companies which continue today, Provident Mutual Life Insurance Company and Provident Trust Company, now Provident National Bank.

JEANES HOSPITAL

In addition to her numerous gifts for Quaker boarding homes and other charities, Anna T. Jeanes left her entire residuary estate to Philadelphia Yearly Meeting to establish and endow "a general hospital or infirmary for cancerous, nervous and disabling ailments."

When opened by Friends in 1929, Jeanes Hospital was entirely for treatment of cancer victims, but it has been transformed since 1946 into a general medical surgical hospital. It is located on the former Jeanes family country estate, Stapeley, in Fox Chase. Over the years additional medical institutions have been located on the Jeanes property including Friends Hall, a Quaker nursing home, American Oncologic Hospital, the Institute for Cancer Research and the Fox Chase Cancer Institute.

On April 7 each year at Jeanes Hospital, violets

JEANES HOSPITAL

and violet corsages are worn by patients and staff members to mark the birthday of the little Quaker lady who contributed so much to her community.

WHARTON SCHOOL OF FINANCE AND COMMERCE

Joseph Wharton, a Quaker industrialist and philanthropist of the Old School, thought universities and colleges ought to teach young people proper management of money and business enterprise. He gave half a million dollars to the University of Pennsylvania in 1881 to establish the first business school in the nation—the Wharton School of Finance and Commerce.

Wharton was a direct descendant of one of William Penn's earliest Quaker settlers. He was chemist, metallurgist, mineralogist, manufacturer and

financier. At 31 he became one of the founders and directors of Saucon Iron Company, which in time became Bethlehem Steel Corporation. He owned and operated a number of industrial enterprises. He accumulated the vast acreage of New Jersey Pine Lands now owned by the Garden State.

Joseph Wharton served as member or chairman of the Board of Managers of Swarthmore College for nearly forty years. He donated the Friends Meeting House located on the campus and gave Swarthmore its first men's dormitory, Wharton Hall.

FRIENDS HISTORICAL LIBRARY, SWARTHMORE COLLEGE

Joseph Wharton's name and a rough drawing of him will appear on a new United States commemorative postage stamp scheduled to be placed on sale at the Wharton School in Philadelphia in June, 1981, in observance of its centennial.

Joseph and Anna Wharton with their family, 1904

THE QUAKER CITY

Most visitors recognize the great statue topping City Hall tower, highest point in Philadelphia's skyline, as that of the Quaker founder, William Penn. Many streets named for prominent Friends also bear witness to Philadelphia's heritage as The Quaker City.

HISTORICAL SOCIETY OF PENNSYLVANIA